The Laws of
Settlements

54 Laws Underlying Settlements
across Scale and Culture

ERICK VILLAGOMEZ

Copyright © 2018, Erick Villagomez

All rights reserved. No part of this book may be reproduced in any form by any electronic or mechanical means (including photocopying recording, or information storage and retrieval) without permission from the author.

Designed by Erick Villagomez

Cover image: Cairo, Egypt and the Nile River. Courtesy of Point Two Design ©EarthStar Geographics

To KIM, my incredible, supportive wife without whom I could never have written this book.

To SOPHIA and SEBASTIAN, who inspire me in every way and to whom the future of our settlements belong.

To the COUNTLESS UNNAMED PEOPLE who incrementally shaped and improved our settlements through simple trial-and-error: we are indebted to your humble actions.

To the late CONSTANTINOS DOXIADIS, whose rigourous and visionary work will undoubtedly be rediscovered.

And of course, to MOM and DAD.

BARCELONA, SPAIN

Table of Contents

INTRODUCTION 13

THE OVERARCHING LAW 25

0. *Human settlements are scalar and co-dependent.* 26

LAWS OF DEVELOPMENT 31

CREATION

1. *Human settlements are the product of different forces and serve to satisfy the human needs of inhabitants and others..32*

2. *Once created, unforeseen functions and needs must be satisfied, over and above initial ones. These grow with the development of the settlement.* 35

3. *The goal of settlement is to satisfy the needs and desires of its inhabitant, particularly those related to happiness and core physical needs, such as clean water and safety..* 36

4. *Fulfilling the needs of those who live in settlements extend beyond core physical needs to social, political, economic and cultural spheres of life..* 39

5. *Human settlements are the created and maintained by their inhabitants..* 41

6. *Settlements are created only when they are needed and live only as long as they are needed—that is, as long as they are satisfying the needs of the forces placed upon them..* 44

DEVELOPMENT

7. *The development and renewal of settlements is a continuous process. If it stops, conditions for its death are created, but how long it will take depends on many factors..* 48

8. *The survival of a settlement is greatly influenced by its geography and role within its larger co-dependent system.* 51

9. *The total investment across all facets of settlement life—economic, social, cultural, etc.—depends on the role it plays within the larger co-dependent settlement system, and the forces being placed on it by this system..* 53

10. *The values created in a settlement, in addition to the initial needs leading to its creation, act as 'secondary forces' contributing to its speedier development; or in case of depression, they slow down or even arrest and reverse its decline. The process is continual, adding different forces intermittently over the lifetime of a settlement.*...................55

11. *In a growing system of settlements the chances are that the largest settlements will grow faster than the others.*...........58

12. *The per capita cost of a settlement's infrastructure decreases in relation to the size of the settlement - the doubling the size of a particular settlement decreases the cost of infrastructure by approx. 15%).*...........................59

13. *Settlements are in a constant state of adaptation and, as such, time is a factor necessary for the development of settlements and is physically expressed within them.*............61

14. *Considerations around speed are indispensable to the understanding and design of settlements.*........................64

EXTINCTION

15. *The gradual death of a settlement begins when the settlement no longer serves and satisfies some of the basic needs of the its inhabitants or of the Society, in general. As people move they carry their values with them.*...................70

16. *The death process of all or part of a settlement will not occur until its initial value has been amortized from the economic and cultural points of view.*............................72

17. *In the death process of a settlement, its elements do not die simultaneously. The same holds true for the values that it represents. As a consequence, the settlement as a whole has much greater chances of surviving and developing through renewal, even if some of its elements are dying.*..........75

18. *During the process of death, inertia caused by existing forces, especially buildings, plays a very important role in slowing down—or even reversing—the process.*...................78

19. *The death process of a settlement is complete when every reason for its life has ceased to exist and/or when the needs it fulfilled within its larger system can be provided elsewhere to a better degree and/or with easier access.*............80

20. The creation, development and death of settlements follow certain laws unless humans decide otherwise..............82

LAWS OF INTERNAL BALANCE — 85

21. The elements in each part of a settlement tend toward balance..86

22. The balance among the elements of a settlement is dynamic balance..87

23. The balance of the elements is expressed in different ways in each phase of the creation and evolution of a settlement. 89

24. The balance between the elements is expressed differently at each scale of a settlement, while each scale interacts dynamically with others.................................90

25. Across all scales of settlement, achieving balance within the range of the human scale is critically important for its long-term success. This scale corresponds to the extents of ones control, as well as the body and senses— roughly a ten minute walking distance..........................92

LAWS OF PHYSICAL CHARACTERISTICS — 97

LOCATION

26. The geographic/topographic location of a settlement depends on the needs it must serve for itself (its inhabitants, natural setting, etc.) and the larger co-dependent settlement system to which it belongs............................98

27. The geographic/topographic location of a settlement depends on its needs, geology, anticipated physical size and technology available. 100

SIZE

28. The population size of a settlement depends on its roles in serving certain needs for its inhabitant and for its larger settlement system..106

29. *The physical size of a settlement depends on its population size, its needs, culture (technology, etc.), its role within the larger settlement system, and its geographic, topographic, climatic, and geologic conditions.* 109

FUNCTIONS

30. *The functions of a settlement depend on the geographic and topographic location, geologic conditions, technological development, population size, and the role within the larger settlement system.* 114

31. *The role of a settlement within its larger co-dependent system depends on its function, geographic/topographic location and population size.* 116

32. *The functions and role of a settlement are interdependent with geography, topographic conditions, geological circumstance, as well as population and physical size.* 117

STRUCTURE

33. *The basic cell of human settlement is a physical scalar unit that is an expression of its community—politically, socially, culturally, economically, etc. The settlement will only function properly only if this unit is not fragmented in any way.* 122

34. *All communities, and therefore, all settlement scalar units tend to be connected to each other hierarchically. Every community of a higher order serves a certain number of communities of a lower order, and the same is true of specific functions with each unit.* 123

35. *The fact that all communities tend to be connected in a hierarchical manner does not mean that this connection is an exclusive one. Many other connections at the same level or at different ones are equally possible, but for organizational purposes the connection is hierarchical.* 126

36. *The existence or creation of communities and functions of a higher order does not necessarily mean the elimination of those of the lower one.* 128

37. *The types of services and satisfaction provided by a settlement's scale, community and function of a higher order to those of a lower order, depend on cost-distance and time-distance.*..130

38. *The overall physical texture of a human settlement depends on its scale and the smaller components of which it is composed.*...132

39. *The texture of a human settlement changes as its dimensions change.*..134

FORM

40. *The main force which shapes human settlements physically is centripetal—that is, the inward tendency towards a close interrelationship of all its parts.*................140

41. *Although the centripetal force at play ideally appears as settlements of concentric circles, the ultimate forms of settlements are conditioned by curves of equal effort defined dominantly by physical exertion, time, and money. These, in turn are influenced by related factors such as geography, geology, topography, and technology.*................141

42. *Linear forces lead to the formation of linear parts of settlements; under certain conditions, this may lead to a linear form of the entire settlement for a certain length only, and after a certain period of time.*.........................145

43. *Undetermined forces, usually caused by the form of the landscape, lead to the formation of settlements of undetermined form.*..146

44. *The form of a settlement is determined by a combination of central, linear, and undetermined forces in adjustment to the landscape and in accordance with its positive and negative characteristics.*...........................149

45. *A settlement grows in the areas of the greatest attraction and least resistance.*.................................151

46. *A factor with a direct impact on the form of a settlement is the need for security which may, at times, be even more important than the main centripetal force.*...........152

47. *Another force that exercises an influence on the form of a settlement is the tendency towards an orderly pattern.......154*

48. *The final form of the settlement depends on the total sum of the forces already mentioned, as well as others such as tradition and cultural factors, which play a greater role in the smaller scales. The final form is a result of the interplay of these primary, secondary, and tertiary forces........157*

49. *The form of the settlement is satisfactory only if all the forces of varying importance within it, can be brought into balance physically..159*

50. *The right form for a human settlement is that which best expresses all the static positions and dynamic movements of humans, animals and machines within its space, while ensuring a healthy ecological setting...............160*

51. *The right form is that which expresses the importance, class, and consequently, the relative scale of every scalar settlement unit and their subdivisions..........................162*

52. *The densities in a settlement, or in any of its parts, depend on the forces which are exercised upon it...............165*

53. *In human settlements formed by a normal process, the pattern of densities changes in a rational and continuous way, according to the scale of the settlement and the functions it serves...168*

54. *The satisfaction derived from the services provided by a settlement to its inhabitants depends greatly on the proper density of the settlement.................................170*

EPILOGUE	**173**
BIBLIOGRAPHY	**183**
INDEX	**193**

ARRAS, FRANCE

Introduction

This book outlines the laws underlying human settlements of all sizes and across all cultures. Within this context, a "settlement" refers to the physical container created to house human activities, one that interacts with the natural environment and artificial constructs over time. Settlements also exist across scales, spanning the smallest group of buildings to the vast cities we see today. This is particularly relevant now, as written works focus on 'urban' landscapes, neglecting to recognize that cities are just one of the many possible stages of human settlements.

My position is straightforward: I believe that, in order to truly understand cities, one must understand the repetitive framework inherent to settlements across scales and developmental stages. To give a physiological analogy, adulthood cannot be truly appreciated without understanding childhood and adolescence. Similarly, cities cannot be well understood without comprehending other settlements such as towns and villages. Furthermore, like human developmental divisions, settlement 'categories' are ambiguous. When does a village become a town? Or a town become a city? At a very basic level, this makes understanding a wider range of settlements critical.

What makes understanding settlements more significant is that, unlike humans, they can pass through different stages indefinitely. That is, their development is not linear from birth to death. Cities can transform to towns and villages as easily as villages and towns can change to cities. This, in theory, can occur in perpetuity. The many Roman cities that transformed into smaller settlements following the fall of the Empire, and subsequently transformed into contemporary global cities, demonstrate this process. This being the case, we would be negligent in focusing too much on any single phase of settlement development—cities and villages, alike—without recognizing their attributes as part of a larger continuum.

Given the breadth required to engage settlements as a whole, comprehensive studies on the subject are few and far between. This is where the work of Constantinos Doxiadis comes in.

Constantino Doxiadis and The Laws of Settlements

The 1960s and 70s were critical for research related to settlements. The reasons for this are varied and complex, but these decades put forth many seminal works in settlement studies. A small sampling will serve to demonstrate the unquestionable richness of this era. Consider Lewis Mumford's influential *The City in History: Its Origins, Its Transformations, and Its Prospects* (1961), that described the development of cities in response to the natural environment and the "urban drama" of its inhabitants. His sentiments resonate with Jane Jacobs' *Death and Life of Great American Cities* (1961), that challenged the established modern planning regime and described the subtleties of how cities work 'on the ground' as a living network of human relationships. A year prior, the influential *Image of the City* by Kevin Lynch (1960) clarified how people perceive the built environment through mental maps. Any urbanist of merit would also mention the incredibly ambitious *A Pattern Language* (1977) by Christopher Alexander and Company from Berkley's Centre for Environmental Structure—that put forth 253 'timeless' patterns that cut across scale and culture—as well as Rem Koolhaas' now-mythical *Delirious*

New York: A Retroactive Manifesto for Manhattan (1978), the critical social and architectural analysis of New York that radically altered the architecture and urban design professions, and whose influence continues to this day.

These works alone are enough to warrant labeling those decades as a golden age of insights around human settlements, but I beg your indulgence by adding a few more for good measure: Aldo Rossi's *The Architecture of the City* (1966), Robert Venturi and Denise Scott Brown's *Learning from Las Vegas* (1972), Edward T. Hall's *The Hidden Dimension* (1966), and Gordon Cullen's *Townscape* (1961), Jan Gehl's Life Between Buildings (1971), Henri Lefebvre's sharp *The Production of Space* (1974), and Oscar Newman's *Defensible Space* (1972). Each of these continues to be extremely influential in their respective fields.

Needless to say, this was an extraordinary time….. and among these icons one must place Greek architect and planner, Constantinos Apostolou Doxiadis. Best known for his planning of Islamabad, Pakistan, his life was sadly cut short in 1975 by Lou Gehrig's disease at the age of 62. At the height of his popularity, his face blessed the cover of Time Magazine, with work spanning 40 countries. A prolific writer, the last decade of his life saw Doxiadis author no less than 7 comprehensive books, as well as various journal articles, that shared his research findings on settlements: research based on cutting edge computer technologies of the time.

He was a pioneer; the first to propose a science of human settlements founded on his theory of "ekistics". This urge towards formalizing a science of settlements continues today in the works of

CONSTANTINOS APOSTOLOU DOXIADIS, 1967. COURTESY JEFF GOODE VIA TORONTO STAR PHOTO ARCHIVE.

those such as Michael Batty (*The New Science of Cities*, 2013) and Serge Salat (*Cities and Forms: On Sustainable Urbanism*, 2012). Curiously, despite his significant contributions to the understanding of settlements, his name and work faded into obscurity after his passing.

Of particular relevance here is Doxiadis' 1968 book, named after the discipline he founded—*Ekistics: An Introduction to the Science of Human Settlements*. It was written in response to the increasing complexity and growth of settlements at that time, and within it, he lays the framework for his work and research. A colossal undertaking, the book required an interdisciplinary and scalar approach, drawing on knowledge from diverse but related fields—such as archeology, geography, ecology and urban planning—and applying it to the understanding of not only cities, but human settlements as a whole—from towns and villages to cities and megacities.

The book, itself—a dense 527 page tome aimed at an academic audience—is one of the first attempts at a rigorously integrated and comprehensive approach to settlements and their associated patterns. And hidden within, with a scant 28 pages dedicated to it, are "54 Ekistic Laws of Settlements". Intentionally simple—explained by only a handful of sentences—their complexity lay in the fact that they cross-referenced one another, creating an intricate and layered understanding of settlements: a very contemporary approach towards the built environment. In keeping with Doxiadis' 'ekistic' approach, the laws applied to all settlements across time and scale, and had 'indisputable' validity based on his exhaustive research.

It was almost a decade and a half ago, at the early stages of my professional and professorial career focusing on settlement patterns, that I was first introduced to this book. I remember the moment vividly: upon discussing the challenge of defining the similarities of settlements across time and culture, a senior colleague—one that would eventually be the closest I ever had to a mentor—casually stated that Doxiadis "pretty much 'figured it out' decades ago." Having never heard of his name before then, I immediately purchased a used copy of *Ekistics* and made my way through the dauntingly large book.

The book was dry and often opaque—much different than the popular titles of Jacobs, Alexander, Lynch and the others that became so influential—but this was outweighed by moments of brilliance and lucid insight. *Ekistics* was, in many ways, ahead of its time, and I implicitly and explicitly refer to its many lessons to this day. But the "54 Laws" specifically resonated with me ever since I first read them.

Maybe it was the sheer audacity of the claim that 'indisputable' laws governing all settlements could be known. Many questions followed: was this the ultimate act of recklessness or bravery? Complete naivety or utter genius? If these were the equivalent of finding the DNA of settlements, why were they treated as a trivial aside in his book, with minimal explanation? The Laws seemed to leave more questions than answers.....with one that particularly nagged at me: After decades of research advances in the field, radical urbanization, and technological advancement, were Doxiadis' "54 Laws of Settlements" still relevant today?

At that point in my career, I was not in the position to say. But from that time on, I used the Laws as

BEIJING, CHINA

an approach and reference to researching and understanding the underlying framework of settlements from around the world. Many individual studies and classes I held over the past decade put them to the test, and amazingly, most have proven exceedingly resilient.

Now, after over a decade of practice, research and teaching focused on settlements big and small, as we all grapple to find solutions to the creation of human settlements across the globe, I believe it is the right time to revive and refresh Doxiadis' "54 Laws".

Simply put: *The Laws of Settlements* outlines Doxiadis' original 54 laws, explaining and updating them in light of the vast amount of accumulated knowledge gained since their original publication. With the addition of nuances when necessary, the underlying motivation is to translate them for the 21st century.

Audience and Organization

Within *Ekistics*, Doxiadis was adamant about the need for research on human settlements to be made accessible to the public. He was well aware that changes in human settlements had a direct connection to the values of its inhabitants. As such, *The Laws of Settlements* is written to act as a shared resource to facilitate the meaningful interaction between top-down and bottom-up parties who design, shape and plan human settlements. It is also written for students of urban planning, urban design, architecture and landscape architecture.

Doxiadis' original approach of having laws that are individually simple and cross-referenced has been maintained. This is supplemented, however, with the inclusion of various easy-to-relate-to precedents, as well as explicit references to seminal works—past and present—outside of Doxiadis' research. This is where readers can dig more deeply into the subject in question, if desired.

Aside from the differences around referencing, and in recognition of the strength of the initial work by Doxiadis, I have stayed true to his expectations. He states that the laws should be "true, helpful, general, and simple" and my revisions maintain the same focus. All amendments are clearly stated.

I also stay true to the format published in *Ekistics*—stating each Law, followed by a succinct description of a few of paragraphs. As mentioned above, these are supplemented with further readings, with the explicit intention of giving readers a starting point to investigate the subject discussed.

A few words about numbering. In keeping with the book's content, each Law is numbered. In the words of Doxiadis: "...not because I consider that this is necessarily their order—although a reasonable order has been attempted—but mainly in order to introduce a proper system of reference."

There is one exception, however. The *Overarching Law* (*Law 0*) is an addition to the original 54. It effectively summarizes the principal idea of *Ekistics*—that human settlements are scalar and co-dependent. This served as a basis for his 54 Laws, and was comprehensively explained in the few hundred pages leading up to them. As such, it requires inclusion right at the outset.

With respect to organizational structure, Doxiadis divided his laws into three sections that are also maintained here: the first, called *The Laws of Development*, deals with the life-cycle of human settlements—how they "are born, develop and die". It is divided into subsections on *Creation, Development* and *Extinction*, accordingly.

The second section—titled *Laws of Internal Balance*—focuses on how settlements achieve balance internally, in order to survive. *The Laws of Physical Characteristic*, the third and final section, deals with more concrete issues and is divided into *Location, Size, Functions, Structure* and *Form*.

Final Thoughts

Henry Glassie once said that "History is not the past. History is a story about the past, told in the present and designed to be useful in constructing the future." This captures the spirit of *The Laws of Settlements*. My translation of Doxiadis' original "54 Ekistic Laws of Settlements" are presented here to be useful in constructing our own future, one that is as uncertain now as it was when they were originally published over 50 years ago.

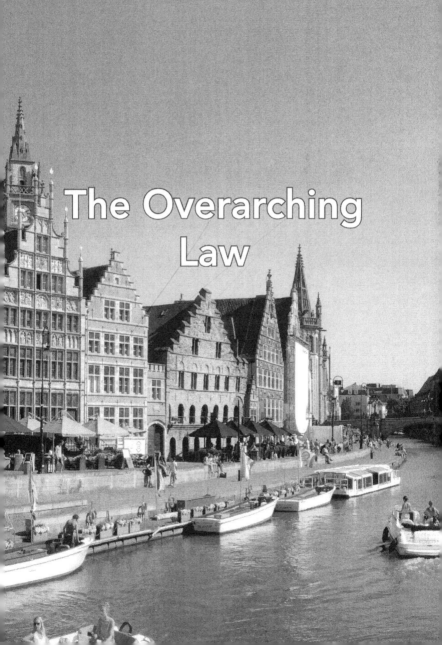

The Overarching Law

0. Human settlements are scalar and co-dependent.

One of the fundamental bases, if not *the* fundamental basis, of Doxiadis' *Ekistics* is that settlements do not exist in isolation. Rather, they are accompanied by other settlements of different shapes and sizes, all of which play different roles. This was not an official "law" within his set of *54 Ekistic Laws of Settlements*, however, he considered it a building block of human settlements as a whole. It was explained in-depth in the chapters preceding his description of the laws, serving as a constant reference and baseline. As such, it requires inclusion here as an overarching law.

To summarize succinctly, Doxiadis determined that human settlements contained what he referred to as "units," ranging from the human body to cities of millions of people. He defined 15 units, grouping them within 4 categories: *minor shells* or *elementary units* included humans, rooms and houses, while *micro settlements* included units smaller than, or the same size as, traditional walkable towns. *Meso settlements*, on the other hand, ranged between walkable towns and "conurbations" (urban environments of up to 14 million people), while the final category—*macro-settlements*—expanded from the latter to the largest unit he called the *Ecumenopolis*, effectively an urban environment of continental proportions with a population of 30,000,000,000.

Specific divisions aside, the essence of Doxiadis' insights is that human settlements are part of a co-dependent scalar system or network—units that work together to form a more complex whole. This has been elaborated on by several writers since. At the most basic level, it is evident in the great number of cities that have been formed by small villages or towns that have gradually expanded into one another or have been more formally acquired through annexation. Recent developments in transportation technology and aviation have allowed this co-dependence to span larger distances.

Henri Pirenne's seminal work *Medieval Cities: Their Origins and the Revival of Trade* is worth mentioning here. Written originally in 1969, the book describes the intricate relationship between different trading settlements across the Mediterranean Sea and their dramatic transformations from dynamic 'international' urban centres to rural-based, localized settlements with weak economies after those co-dependent ties were severed.

Many more recent, seminal works also speak to this idea. In *A Pattern Language*, for example, Christopher Alexander orders his 'patterns' according to scale, from largest to smallest—region to room. He states: "Each pattern is connected to certain 'larger' patterns which come above it in the language; and to certain 'smaller' patterns which come below it in the language. The pattern helps to complete those larger patterns which are 'above' it, and is itself completed by those smaller patterns which are below it."

Mark DeKay and G.Z. Brown build from this idea in their excellent work *Sun, Wind and Light: Architectural Design Strategies*, furthering the initial scalar idea by adding connections to environmental systems, both passive and active. More specifically, how issues related to climate—"sun for heating, wind for cooling, and daylight for natural lighting"—affect buildings and built form. Its strategies range from building groupings through individual buildings and buildings elements (windows, floors, walls, etc.), tying these to larger patterns.

Similarly, in his rigorous research of settlements across the Appalachians—*East 40 Degrees: An Interpretive Atlas*—Jack Williams describes how towns "...with their infrastructure exist as a network across the landscape; the way they are connected implies a larger order."

At the neighbourhood scale, Anne Vernez Moudon's in-depth study of the built fabric around Alamo Square in San Francisco explicitly addresses cities as scalar organisms. In *Built for Change*, she explicitly describes the physical structure of the city as a series of interrelated scales ranging from topography, through street networks, blocks, buildings, and rooms—each of which is intricately explained in detail.

More recently, Jonathan Rose's succinct history of how cities developed over time, in *The Well-Tempered City*, cites connectivity as one of the nine fundamental characteristics necessary for the emergence of the first cities. Speaking to the early Ubaid period of settlement development, from 5500 to 4000 BCE, he states "The connectivity of differentiated communities, and the commerce and culture that flowed through them, enriched the network effect that not only increased the diversity of the whole system, but allowed each community to increase its own diversity." This laid the foundation for larger settlements to develop and is, accordingly, a critical trait of their success.

This is just a small sampling of the diverse writing that has supported Doxiadis' scalar approach to human settlements and their co-dependence. This can easily expand to include the works of Serge Salat, Nikos Salingaros and Renee Chow, to name a few more. Although they do not necessarily name the same specific "units" as Doxiadiss, the overarching idea around the interconnection of settlements across scales and space remains front-and-centre. And in an era of global reach, it remains more valid than ever before.

FURTHER READING:
- **Constantino Doxiadis** - *Ekistics: The Science of Human Settlements*
- **Henri Pirenne** - *Medieval Cities: Their Origins and the Revival of Trade*
- **Christopher Alexander** - *A Pattern Language*
- **Jack Williams** - *East 40 Degrees: An Interpretive Atlas*
- **Mark DeKay and G.Z. Brown** - *Sun, Wind and Light - Architectural Design Strategies*
- **Anne Vernez Moudon** - *Built of Change: Neighbourhood Architecture in San Francisco*
- **Jonathan F. P. Rose** - *The Well-Tempered City*
- **Renee Chow** - *Suburban Space: The Fabric of Dwelling*
- **Nikos A. Salingaros** - *Principles of Urban Structure*
- **Jane Jacobs** - *The Nature of Economies*
- **Spiro Kostof** - *The City Shaped*

SAN FRANCISCO, UNITED STATES OF AMERICA

1
Laws of Development

CREATION

1. Human settlements are the product of different forces and serve to satisfy the human needs of inhabitants and others.

Settlements are born from human needs. Satisfying core physical needs—such as access to clean water, air, food and physical safety (*Law 3*)—are critical starting points. However, given that settlements also facilitate human interactions, they are created to accommodate and formalize collective values, desires and requirements. In the words of Kevin Lynch, "The form of a settlement is always willed and valued, but its complexity and its inertia frequently obscure those connections."

Lynch's quote speaks well to the complex, diverse forces and needs that give birth to settlements, and one of the most obvious forces revolves around the natural context (*Laws 31-32*). In the Pulitzer Prize winning book *Guns Germs and Steel*, for example, Jared Diamond shows how geography and conditions that were favourable to agriculture led to the birth of a number of civilizations and their respective settlements. These civilizations, in turn, created technologies, social institutions, immunities to diseases and other cultural phenomena that led to certain societies overtaking others.

Economic forces, such as trade, are also clear drivers in the creation and development of settlements. For example, if a number of towns require a large market centre to serve them, a settlement may be created in an area that best suits this purpose. Trade, moreover, is often associated with access and transportation, with the birth of countless historical settlements occurring at the intersection of major roads and along trade routes, such as the Silk Road.

History is also filled with examples of settlements created by other forces: military, religious, administrative, and/or cosmological forces, to name just a few more. This brings to mind William Morrish's poetic verbal and visual description of how earth and mountain "evoked powerful spiritual and civic actions resulting in the inauguration of the basic formal and spatial framework of an urban terrain; cities which grow from landform."

Regardless of what forces are driving the creation of settlements, however, the fact remains that all aspects of settlement are steered by human needs and desires. This law is summarized well in Janet Abu-Lughod's "The Islamic City": "Cities are the products of many forces, and the forms that evolve in response to these forces are unique to the combination of those forces."

FURTHER READING:
- **Constantino Doxiadis** - *Ekistics: The Science of Human Settlements*
- **Kevin Lynch** - *Good City Form*
- **Jared Diamond** - *Guns Germs and Steel*
- **Anthony E.J. Morris** - *History of Urban Form: Before the Industrial Revolution*
- **Paul Knox** - *Atlas of Cities*
- **William Rees Morrish** - *Civilizing Terrains: Mountains, Mounds and Mesas*
- **Darran Anderson** - *Imaginary Cities*
- **Besim Selim Hakim** - *Arabic-Islamic Cities*
- **Janet Abu-Lughod**, "The Islamic City: Historic Myths, Islamic Essence, and Comtemporary Relevance" from *International Journal of Middle East Studies* (**1987**)
- **Jonathan F. P. Rose** - *The Well-Tempered City*

34   **CHAPTER** : Laws of Development - Creation

DEHLI, INDIA

2. Once created, unforeseen functions and needs must be satisfied, over and above initial ones. These grow with the development of the settlement.

As outlined in *Law 1*, settlements are created around specific needs and desires. As time passes, however, they evolve to develop other unexpected functions and purposes that supplement the originals—sometimes overtaking them entirely. Like the initial needs themselves, new potential functions are extremely diverse. The development of industrial, technological, administrative and/or cultural roles are some of the more common.

As populations grow, original and unpredicted functions become fodder for the further development of complexity and diversity of needs (*Law 4*). This, in turn, increases the chances that early purposes will be replaced, and affect the rate at which this occurs. Such is the case with the many cities, villages and towns founded by the Roman Empire that are thriving today, including Barcelona, Istanbul and Vienna.

It's important to note that, although it is often believed that growth and increasing complexity are a positive attribute of settlements, these same forces can bring with them the seeds of destruction. Joseph Tainter's central argument in his seminal work *The Collapse of Complex Societies*, for example, describes various instances—from the Western Roman Empire to the Maya—where increased complexity carried with it "increased costs per capita" that ultimately reach a point of decreasing returns. Tainter's insight that "Complex societies historically are vulnerable to collapse..." is worth pondering now more than ever before, given the rate of change and transformation at all levels of society.

FURTHER READING:
- **Constantino Doxiadis** - *Ekistics: The Science of Human Settlements*
- **Anthony E.J. Morris** - *History of Urban Form: Before the Industrial Revolution*
- **Paul Knox** - *Atlas of Cities*
- **Joseph Tainter** - *The Collapse of Complex Societies*

3. The goal of settlement is to satisfy the needs and desires of its inhabitant, particularly those related to happiness and core physical needs, such as clean water and safety.

Satisfying core physical needs—such as access to clean air, water, food, and protection from harm—are known to be the foundations of all settlements. In fact, some of the largest building feats in history have revolved around the latter, from the Roman aqueducts to the Three Gorges Dam, the Great Wall of China to the Hollandic Water Lines.

At a smaller scale, fortified and walled settlements are central figures in history, appearing in the earliest known permanent built environments. The "old walled city", for example, is one of the three basic parts of the Mesopotamian city-state of Ur as described by Anthony Morris in his comprehensive *History of Urban Form: Before the Industrial Revolution*. Although defensive walls have disappeared from many contemporary settlements, issues of safety remain at the forefront, be it through policing, CCTV surveillance cameras or the creation of "defensible space" neighbourhoods.

CHAPTER : Laws of Development - Creation **37**

SEGOVIA, SPAIN

In *Good City Form*, Kevin Lynch defines the core needs he believes are required for a good living environment, grouping them within what he calls "Vitality". Individually, the components of the latter are "Sustenance" (adequate supply of food, energy, water, etc.), "Safety" (an environment that minimizes physical harm, disease, poisons, etc.) and "Consonance" (optimizing sensory input in keeping with natural rhythms, etc.). These core needs, he argues, are the essential building blocks of sustaining human life and necessarily contribute to human happiness.

Discussions around happiness have been ongoing for millennia. As captured by Aristotle's often repeated statement "Happiness is the meaning and the purpose of life, the whole aim and end of human existence," the issue has been central to the development of different societies across time around the globe. Similarly, scholarship and discussion around the relationship between settlements and happiness have been continuous.

Recent developments in the understanding of happiness and research into cities have coalesced into a better understanding of the relationship between settlements and their effects on one's psychological well-being. That the design of settlements strongly influences the moods and behaviours of their inhabitants is not necessarily new, but its grounding in research has grown drastically in recent decades, with popular books such as Charles Montgomery's *Happy City* forging a clear path on the issue.

Although one may argue the specific elements of the built environment that create 'happiness',

Montgomery defines it broadly to include *Core Needs* among *Joy, Health, Equity, Ease, Meaning & Belonging, Sociability* and *Resilience*—each of which, he believes, can and should be manifested in the design of the built environment.

FURTHER READING:
- **Constantino Doxiadis** - *Ekistics: The Science of Human Settlements*
- **Clemens Steenbergen, Johan van der Zwart and Joost Grootens** - *Atlas of the New Dutch Water Defence Line*
- **Anthony E.J. Morris** - *History of Urban Form: Before the Industrial Revolution*
- **Oscar Newman** - *Defensible Space*
- **Kevin Lynch** - *Good City Form*
- **Charles Montgomery** - *Happy City: Transforming Our Live Through Urban Design*

4. Fulfilling the needs of those who live in settlements extend beyond core physical needs to social, political, economic and cultural spheres of life.

The success and survival of settlements over time depends on moving beyond basic physical needs to provide meaning and purpose. As introduced in *Law 3*, Charles Montgomery's 'Elements of Happiness'— based on the comprehensive research in *Happy City*—are helpful here and include *Core Needs, Joy, Health, Equity, Ease, Meaning & Belonging, Sociability* and *Resilience*. It is evident that these elements cut across social, political, economic and cultural spheres of life.

With this in mind, Doxiadis puts forth the idea that the survival of settlements over time requires

40 **CHAPTER** : Laws of Development - Creation

BEIJING, CHINA

a dynamic balance (*Law 21-22*) across these components. It is important to note that he defines balance as a *range* within tolerable limits, and not a definitive target. Furthermore, he argues that a failure to achieve this balance creates instability within the system and conditions that can lead to the death of a settlement.

Although this law highlights a number of important factors, one of the most significant is the fallacy of claiming the significance of a single sphere over others. In the contemporary world, it is common to judge and plan settlements according to economic indicators and measures alone. As a single facet of a complex set of human needs to be met, Doxiadis would argue that this approach is insufficient.

FURTHER READING:
- **Constantino Doxiadis** - *Ekistics: The Science of Human Settlements*
- **Charles Montgomery** - *Happy City: Transforming Our Live Through Urban Design*

5. Human settlements are the created and maintained by their inhabitants.

It is clear that the initial creation of settlements can be, and have been, created by external agents—be it institutions or governments. It is also evident that the labour behind the initial physical construction of a human settlement is not necessarily done by those who live in them—the largely transient labour market that serves as the foundation of China's recent rapid development, is a strong contemporary example. However, this law states that the long-term success and survival of settled landscapes correspond to those who are willing to dwell in and maintain them over time, both economically and physically.

One of the most influential writers of the past century on the subject was Jane Jacobs, who described the subtle and 'complex order' between city inhabitants and their built environments. Her keen observations within *The Death and Life of Great American Cities* about store owners who maintained the life of the street socially and physically clearly demonstrates this at the smaller scale of inhabitation. This is echoed in her often repeated quote: "Cities have the capability of providing something for everybody, only because, and only when, they are created by everybody."

Allan B. Jacobs' wonderful 'visual diagnoses' described within *Looking at Cities* elaborates on Jane Jacobs' sensibilities, speaking to issues around maintenance of buildings and their implications as potential indicators of social change in an area. Unlike Jane Jacobs, however, he is interested in what these physical changes mean and the ties between the social, economic and physical fabric of urban settlements.

In *How Building Learn*, Stewart Brand addresses this issue from yet another angle, introducing the idea that different elements of the built environment that relate to different scales—"Stuff", "Space Plan","Services","Skin","Structure" and "Site"—change at different rates. Accordingly, each element is affected, transformed and maintained by different agents based on their complexity and scale. Thus, furniture—or "Stuff"—is typically used and maintained directly by its users, while "Site" (legally defined lots and boundaries) is affected by a different series of agents.

This is related to issues of control and controlling agents, a topic N.J. Habraken's *Structure of the Ordinary* addresses well. In his words: "Whenever physical parts are introduced, displaced, or removed from a site, some controlling agent—a person, group of persons, organization or institution—is revealed. Control thus defines the central operational relationship between humans and all matter that is the stuff of the built environment. As dynamic patterns of change echo throughout the built environment, they reveal the structure of control. In light of the built environment's organic patterns of growth and change, and the transformational 'behavior' of its forms, it appears to act very much as a living whole."

Despite the different approaches and focuses of each author, the fact that inhabitants continuously create and maintain their respective settlements is explicitly stated or readily assumed to be evident. We all partake in this process everyday.

FURTHER READING:
- **Constantino Doxiadis** - *Ekistics: The Science of Human Settlements*
- **Rem Koolhaas** - *GSD Project on the City I - Great Leap Forward*
- **Jane Jacobs** - *The Death and Life of Great American Cities*
- **Allan B. Jacobs** - *Looking At Cities*
- **Stewart Brand** - *How Building Learn: What Happens After They're Built*
- **N.J. Habraken** - *Structure of The Ordinary*

6. Settlements are created only when they are needed and live only as long as they are needed—that is, as long as they are satisfying the needs of the forces placed upon them.

Given that human settlements are created to fulfill the needs of their inhabitants and the diverse forces acting on them (*Laws 1-4*), it's clear that once those needs are no longer satisfied, the settlement can be vacated and/or destroyed. As discussed in *Laws 3-4*, the needs to be met cut across physical, social, political, economic and cultural spheres. Instability within, or across, any of these can lead to the desolation and/or elimination of a settlement. The many resource-based 'ghost towns' around the world that are vacated after resources are depleted are an explicit example of this process.

The Goggles' award-winning *Welcome to Pine Point* web documentary that explores the erasure of the former mining town of Pine Point in the Northwest Territories of Canada, speaks particularly well to the impacts of this process and how human lives are affected.

FURTHER READING:
- **Constantino Doxiadis** - *Ekistics: The Science of Human Settlements*
- **The Goggles** - *Welcome to Pine Point* - http://pinepoint.nfb.ca/#/pinepoint

CHAPTER : Laws of Development - Creation   **45**

MACHU PICCHU, PERU

RICHMOND, CANADA

DEVELOPMENT

7. The development and renewal of settlements is a continuous process. If it stops, conditions for its death are created, but how long it will take depends on many factors.

The word settlement is often used to describe a physical product, a 'thing' in itself, or a collection of 'things' (i.e. buildings). Now, more than ever before however, it is clear that settlements are processes: a series of actions created by a diversity of people that yields material 'things' in space. What we experience as a settlement day-to-day is a (seemingly) static moment in a dynamic process of necessary and continuous change. This is echoed by Janet Abu-Lughod in "The Islamic City: Historical Myths, Islamic Essence, and Contemporary Relevance" as she describes the socio-cultural processes that affected the creation of traditional Islamic urban form. "A city at one point in time is a still photograph of a complex system of building and destroying, of organizing and reorganizing, and so on." She concludes: "Cities are processes, not products." This applies to all settlements.

Well-known urbanist Kevin Lynch speaks well to this in his attempts to capture the various aspects of settlement form as: "...solely the inert physical thing? Or the living organisms too? The actions people engage in? The social structure? The economic system? The ecological system? The control of the space and its meaning? The way it presents itself to the senses? Its daily and seasonal rhythms? Its secular changes?" He ultimately describes settlements as "...the spatial arrangement of persons

CHAPTER 1: Laws of Development - Development

MACHU PICCHU, PERU

doing things, the resulting spatial flows of persons, goods, and information, and the physical features which modify space in some way significant to those actions, including enclosures, surfaces, channels, ambiences and objects. Further, the description must include the cyclical and secular changes in those spatial distributions, the control of space and the perception of it."

As a result, if the process of settlement stops, conditions that can lead to its death ensue. However, the amount of time required for a settlement to die varies greatly—depending on a diversity of factors, discussed later in *Extinction* (*Laws 16-21*).

Regardless, the inability to understand settlements as processes of continual change has many important implications. For example, the perception that a settlement is the sole result of static physical 'objects' such as houses, schools, or cars, can lead to false expectations, errors in judgement, and flawed attempts to prevent change from occurring. Worse still, it can prevent measures that foster the successful and/or healthy development of a settlement. The worst cases of NIMBYism fall under this category.

REFERENCES:
- **Constantino Doxiadis** - *Ekistics: The Science of Human Settlements*
- **Janet Abu-Lughod** - "The Islamic City: Historical Myths, Islamic Essence, and Contemporary Relevance" in International Journal of Middle East Studies (1987)
- **Kevin Lynch** - *Good City Form*
- **Jane Jacobs** - *The Nature of Economies*
- **Stewart Brand** - *How Buildings Learn*

8. The survival of a settlement is greatly influenced by its geography and role within its larger co-dependent system.

Whether a settlement thrives or falters is greatly affected by its geography and relationship to other settlements within its larger co-dependent system (*Law 0*). As summarized by Constantino Doxiadis: "As with all living organisms, the capacity of a settlement for survival depends mainly on its ability to meet competition with similar species...in the same space."

Jared Diamond's convincing argument describing how geography and the conditions favouring agriculture led to the birth of a number of civilizations has already been referred to in *Law 1*. The evolution of certain medieval towns as strong Renaissance cities due to their geographical locations—like those at the intersection of important trade routes, as described by Henri Pirenne in *Medieval Cities*—is another example.

A popular contemporary case is the decline of the North American "Main Street" whereby a large number of local commercial 'high streets' that had evolved in response to old modes of transportation (walking, train, water, etc.) began to decline with the growing popularity of cars, the creation of highways and development of large-scale regional shopping malls.

The aggressive growth of global urban branding initiatives that seek to attract the travellers and tourists from around the globe to specific cities is

OLLANTAYTAMBO, PERU

also a powerful modern example. In fact, many tend to use geography as one of the many incentives to lure people to their doorsteps.

REFERENCES:
- **Constantino Doxiadis** - *Ekistics: The Science of Human Settlements*
- **Jared Diamond** - *Guns Germs and Steel*
- **Henri Pirenne** - *Medieval Cities: Their Origins and the Revival of Trade*
- **James Howard Kunstler** - *The Geography of Nowhere*
- **Rem Koolhaas** - *GSD Project on the City II - Guide to Shopping*

9. The total investment across all facets of settlement life—economic, social, cultural, etc.—depends on the role it plays within the larger co-dependent settlement system, and the forces being placed on it by this system.

In an age of urban branding and rampant city-building, it is certainly no surprise that investment in a settlement is based on its role within its larger co-dependent system (*Law 0*). Although focus often tends to be on the economic or cultural engines of nations—such as New York, Hong Kong, London and Barcelona—it's important to remember that there is an extremely wide range of settlement types. From Resort Municipalities (such as Whistler, BC) to Themed Towns (such as Leavenworth in Washington), each built environment plays a different role in their respective areas.

More recently, Paul Knox notes the contemporary growth of new roles for cities in light of globalization. These roles include being nodes for "transnational corporate organization, international banking and finance, supranational government, and the work of international agencies." Echoes of the latter are found in Keller Easterling's *Extrastatecraft* that describes the proliferation of 'free zone' cities created to jump-start the economies of developing nations through the creation of incentives offered by non-local authorities.

Given the scalar nature of settlements highlighted in *Law 0*, roles are also affected by their scale. In larger settlements, such as cities, different roles can be seen at district, neighbourhood, and street scales. Thus, we see commercial districts, tourist nodes and ethnic clusters, each drawing their own particular forms of investment from inside and outside sources.

Interestingly, Doxiadis highlights that in a balanced condition (*Law 21*), the total investment across all spheres of life within the settlement often corresponds to the total income of its inhabitants. This, he continues, is in equilibrium with the costs needed for food, clothing, education, etc. He recognizes, however, that this isn't always the case where new and/or abandoned areas are being (re)developed. In these circumstances, extensive investment is often required at the outset.

The past few decades, in particular, have seen the proliferation of this condition in places such as China and United Arab Emirates. This is particularly well-described in Stephen Graham's *Vertical: The City from Satellites to Bunkers* and Thomas J. Campanella's *The Concrete Dragon: China's Urban Revolution and What it Means for the World*. It is important to note, however, that the extent of investment is based on the actual or perceived potential of each settlement, as well as its ability to respond to all the forces that are being exerted on it by the larger system.

REFERENCES:
- **Constantino Doxiadis** - *Ekistics: The Science of Human Settlements*
- **Paul Knox** - *Atlas of Cities*
- **Keller Easterling** - *Extrastatecraft: The Power of Infrastructure Space*
- **Stephen Graham** - *Vertical: The City from Satellites to Bunkers*
- **Thomas J. Campanella** - *The Concrete Dragon: China's Urban Revolution and What it Means for the World*

10. The values created in a settlement, in addition to the initial needs leading to its creation, act as 'secondary forces' contributing to its speedier development; or in case of depression, they slow down or even arrest and reverse its decline. The process is continual, adding different forces intermittently over the lifetime of a settlement.

Could a settlement survive the decline of the initial needs and forces that led to its creation? Definitely. The countless settlements that have survived across centuries of change socially, culturally and technologically, speak to this. Rome, Athens, Jericho, Jerusalem, Varansi (India), and Luoyang (China) are just a few. This occurs due to the development of different roles that settlements develop over time.

Doxiadis describes a theoretical example of a harbour town that develops a strong timber shipbuilding industry, and whose harbour begins to suffer from competition by a nearby settlement.

In response, the initial harbour town continues to survive as an industrial town focused on building steel ships—an industry that developed out of the initial timber boat-building activities.

Contemporary examples include the many cities that have given up their industrial tethers for being safe-havens for global capital and speculation—Vancouver, Canada perhaps being a poster child of this process. In these cases, settlement transformations often result in the destruction, replacement and/or re-development of the infrastructure and buildings associated with the earlier outdated uses.

This dynamic process is continuous across the lifetime of a settlement (*Law 7* and *Law 22*). As such, 'secondary' forces are not the end point—tertiary, quaternary, quinary forces, and so on, can develop. The number of additional forces is potentially limitless, as is evident by the ancient settlements that remain active today. The effects of this process have the potential to increase the speed of development and investment, as well as slow down or reverse decline. Henri Pirenne's seminal work outlining the 'direct continuation of the economy of the Roman Empire" via trading through settlements around the Mediterranean Sea after the decline of the Empire, is a case in point.

REFERENCES:
- **Constantino Doxiadis** - *Ekistics: The Science of Human Settlements*
- **Paul Knox** - *Atlas of Cities*
- **Henri Pirenne** - *Medieval Cities: Their Origins and The Revival of Trade*
- **Lewis Mumford** - *The City in History: Its Origins, Its Transformations, and Its Prospects*

CHAPTER 1: Laws of Development - Development

BEIJING, CHINA

11. In a growing system of settlements the chances are that the largest settlements will grow faster than the others.

Doxiadis considers this a "basic law of dynamic systems" based on his initial research showing that "the larger ones attract greater and more functions and grow more than others." Since that time, more research and energy has been put towards exploring this idea. A recent example lies in the research of physicist Geoffrey West around the mathematical scaling laws governing different organisms, including cities. Succinctly summarizing his findings in his 2011 TedTalk "The surprising math of cities and corporations" he states that doubling the size of a particular settlement increases all facets of economic activity (income, construction, etc.) by approximately 15%." That is, cities scale "superlinearly" with respect to socio-economic quantities.

According to his findings, the law is universal, transcending culture and location. In his words "....the bigger you are the more you have per capita, unlike biology—higher wages, more super-creative people per capita as you get bigger, more patents per capita, more crime per capita....If you double the size of a city from 100,000 to 200,000, from a million to two million, 10 to 20 million, it doesn't matter, then systematically you get a 15 percent increase in wages, wealth, number of AIDS cases, number of police, anything you can think of. It goes up by 15 percent...."

West's most recent book, *Scale: The Universal Laws of Growth, Innovation, Sustainability, and the Pace of*

Life in Organisms, Cities, Economies, and Companies, summarizes his findings and applies his insights on the laws of scaling—that is, how complex systems respond as they change in size—to systems beyond cities and settlements.

REFERENCES:
- **Constantino Doxiadis - Ekistics: The Science of Human Settlements**
- **Geoffrey West** - *The Surprising Math of Cities and Corporations* - https://www.ted.com/talks/geoffrey_west_the_surprising_math_of_cities_and_corporations
- **Geoffrey West** - *Scale: The Universal Laws of Growth, Innovation, Sustainability, and the Pace of Life in Organisms, Cities, Economies, and Companies*

12. The per capita cost of a settlement's infrastructure decreases in relation to the size of the settlement - the doubling the size of a particular settlement decreases the cost of infrastructure by approx. 15%)

This is one of the laws that Doxiadis got incorrect, according to recent research. I've rewritten it, accordingly. Although all of his laws were based on his exhaustive research, the limitations of information and data at the time required that certain principles of his be based on "common sense," and this was one of them. His initial convictions stated that "The per capita cost of a settlement increases (other conditions, such as income, being equal) in proportion to the services provided by it and the number of its inhabitants".

WEST VANCOUVER, CANADA

Recent research has shown, however, that increasing the size of settlements decreases the costs associated with it, specifically around infrastructure. The research of Geoffrey West outlined in *Law 11* speaks to this directly, stating that when a settlement doubles in size, it requires an increase in resources of only 85 percent—that is, "you have a 15 percent savings on the infrastructure".

In contrast to socio-economic quantities cited in *Law 11*, settlements scale 'sublinearly' when applied to infrastructure. So, "a city of 10 million people typically needs 15 percent less of the same infrastructure compared with two cities of 5 million each, leading to significant savings in materials and energy use." This is one of the many reasons why dense cities are often labelled more 'sustainable' than their less dense counterparts.

REFERENCES:
- **Geoffrey West** - *The Surprising Math of Cities and Corporations* - https://www.ted.com/talks/geoffrey_west_the_surprising_math_of_cities_and_corporations
- **Geoffrey West** - *Scale: The Universal Laws of Growth, Innovation, Sustainability, and the Pace of Life in Organisms, Cities, Economies, and Companies*

13. Settlements are in a constant state of adaptation and, as such, time is a factor necessary for the development of settlements and is physically expressed within them.

Issues around time are implicitly or explicitly stated in virtually all of Doxiadis' laws. However, this one speaks to the relationship between time and its physical expression within a human settlement. More specifically, he suggests that despite the fact that settlements are dynamic (*Law 7* and *Law 22*), they are often planned as "static" entities, with limited considerations of future conditions. As such, the physical changes made to a settlement embody earlier assumptions made by its inhabitants.

Doxiadis uses the example of highways designed for projected future capacities. In this case, dimensions of time are embedded in the physical fabric of the highway—its width, for example. As time passes, decisions are made in response to those earlier design solutions.

In *Street Fight*, Janette Sadik-Khan and Seth Solomonow describe the process of "re-reading" existing streets and, in doings so, being able to "reallocate the space already there—no expensive reconstruction required." Critically analysing the standard twelve-foot lanes common to North American cities and based on federal highway guidelines, they conclude that the "model street alone may contain more than twenty feet of excess road space not actually needed to move or park vehicles. Multiply that by hundreds of thousands of miles of lanes in thousands of urban areas around the world and you'll find millions of miles of sidewalks, bus and bike lanes, and public spaces—entire cities—trapped within our streets."

Layers of time become more complex as settlements become older. In Barcelona, for example, remnants of the ancient Roman settlement of Barcino remain etched within the contemporary urban fabric. The contemporary city, thus, evolved in response to many of the initial design decisions that structured the early city. This includes a variety of elements, from street orientation to the dimensions of open spaces, as explained so well in Manuel de Solà-Morales' *Ten Lessons on Barcelona*.

By no means is this only evident in old settlements. Even younger ones have a temporal fingerprint. In *Dream City*, for example, Lance Berelowitz describes how the glass towers of Vancouver, Canada resulted from the initial lot and block sizes that have their logic in seventeenth century surveying practices based on the 'rod' and 'chain'.

Similarly, in his brilliant book *Los Angeles Boulevards: Eight X-rays of the Body Public*, Doug Suisman describes how the broad structure of the boulevards in Los Angeles are a consequence of historical circumstances and boundaries of early Spanish settlement patterns rooted in the Laws of the Indies.

Interestingly, the long-term results of this process—as cycles of creation, destruction, obsolescence, replacement and transformation accrete over time—is often the creation of a 'manufactured ground'. As Stephen Graham highlights in *Vertical: The City from Satellites to Bunkers*, "Over centuries, large cities thus literally rise up on ground of their own making. They build their own geology and move up to levels considerably beyond that created by 'natural' stratigraphy...The surface of Rome, which hides many complete ancient worlds, has been built up as much as 15 metres (50 feet) in the last 2,000 years."

REFERENCES:
- **Constantino Doxiadis** - *Ekistics: The Science of Human Settlements*
- **Manuel de Solà-Morales** - *Ten Lessons On Barcelona*
- **Lance Berelowitz** - *Dream City: Vancouver and the Global Imagination*

- **Dora P. Crouch** - *Spanish City Planning in North America*
- **Stephen Graham** - *Vertical: The City from Satellites to Bunkers*
- **John Reps** - *The Making of Urban America: A History of City Planning in the United States*
- **Janette Sadik-Khan & Seth Solomonow** - *Street Fight: Handbook for the Urban Revolution*
- **Anthony E.J. Morris** - *History of Urban Form: Before the Industrial Revolution*
- **Serge Salat** - *Cities and Forms: On Sustainable Urbanism*

14. Considerations around speed are indispensable to the understanding and design of settlements.

Speed and time (*Law 13*) are inherently related. This is clear in their scientific definition: Time=Distance x Speed. This law—worded quite differently than the original put forth by Doxiadis—speaks specifically to the effects of speed on the perception and design of human settlements. That the experience of moving through a settlement is worth consideration was perhaps most popularly captured in the 20th century in Gordon Cullen's *The Concise Townscape*. Cullen developed the concept of 'Serial Vision' and was interested in how people perceived the built environment. He argued that humans understood their surroundings through a "sequence of revelations" that juxtaposed current and emerging views as people moved through a settlement. This, in turn, influenced many others including Besim Hakim who used the same techniques in his thorough analysis of the village of Sidi Bou Sa'id in Tunisia.

Of course, this idea has much older roots, at least as far back as the Athenian Acropolis, where

BEIJING, CHINA

experiences along a guided and gradual procession culminating in the ancient citadel were intentionally created and deemed critical to the understanding of the architecture. Speaking to the main elements that led to the formation of the Periclean Acropolis, Robin Francis Rhodes writes "...there are indications that distinct qualities of procession were transferred directly to the architecture of the Archaic Acropolis, and that they eventually comprised one of the guiding principles of the unified, formalized building program of Pericles." Centuries later, this inspired Le Corbusier's "promenade architecturale".

Recent developments in transportation (automobiles, airplanes, etc.) have altered the perception of the city and, in turn, how it is shaped. Streets designed for horses are much different in size and proportions than those created for automobiles. This fact is clearly captured in Michael Southworth & Eran Ben-Joseph's *Streets and the Shaping of Towns and Cities* that charts the transformation of streets over time.

Perhaps one of the earliest books engaging the subject of perception and speed in the contemporary city is *View from the Road* written by Kevin Lynch and Donald Appleyard. Within, they critically consider the visual experience from inside a fast-moving vehicle on a highway. With this in mind, Doxiadis cites how the 'walking city' results in a more detailed and tactile architecture, while something very different is created by a highway urbanism devoid of "external street decoration."

As a meaningful counterpoint, one can look at the super-sized decoration of the architecture and signs along the Las Vegas Strip—so well described by Robert Venturi and Denise Scott Brown's seminal book *Learning From Las Vegas*. Many of the everyday suburban commercial arterials use similar methods of engaging speed in contemporary settlements.

Present-day built environments are under more pressure than ever to meaningfully engage and understand issues around speed. The ever-increasing diversity of speeds with which people move horizontally and vertically in settlements are clear. Moreover, the wide range of movement technologies—from walking to driving, skateboards to drones, hover boards to bicycles—all have their potential impact on settlements and experience. They, in turn, offer fertile ground for research, discovery and exploration.

REFERENCES:
- **Constantino Doxiadis** - *Ekistics: The Science of Human Settlements*
- **Gordon Cullen** - *The Concise Townscape*
- **Besim Selim Hakim** - *Sidi Bou Sa'id, Tunisia: Structure and Form of a Mediterranean Village*
- **Kevin Lynch** - *Image of the City*
- **Kevin Lynch/Donald Appleyard** - *View from the Road* (**VIDEO:** https://www.youtube.com/watch?v=xP-3maTrQZXE)
- **Robert Venturi, Denise Scott Brown** - *Learning From Las Vegas*
- **Michael Southworth & Eran Ben-Joseph** - *Streets and the Shaping of Towns and Cities*
- **Stephen Graham** - *Vertical: The City from Satellites to Bunkers*
- **Bernard Tschumi** - *Red is not a Colour*
- **Peter Bosselman** - "Images in Motion" in *Representation of Places: Reality and Realism in City Design*
- **J.B. Jackson** - "The Stranger's Path" In *Landscape in Sight*

NORTH VANCOUVER, CANADA

EXTINCTION

15. **The gradual death of a settlement begins when the settlement no longer serves and satisfies some of the basic needs of the its inhabitants or of the Society, in general. As people move they carry their values with them.**

In *Laws 1, 2*, and *11* the intricate relationship between the inhabitants of a settlement and the creation of their built environment in response to their needs was described. These include core physical needs as well as those tied to the social, political, economic and cultural spheres of their lives. By logical extension, a failure to meet some or all of these needs may lead to the process of decline. This is obvious in resource-based towns where, once the resource in question is depleted, the inhabitants move to a different location.

Needs can be more subtle, however. Henri Pirenne's powerful examination of the complex processes and factors that led to the decline and transformation of urban life in the Middle Ages after the fall of the Roman Empire, is a strong case in point. In *Medieval Cities: Their Origins and the Revival of Trade*, he highlights a decline in trade—specifically across the Mediterranean—as a significant factor in the gradual death of a number of significant Roman settlements.

In tandem with the decline of a settlement, Doxiadis importantly states that people take their values with them as they relocate. Since settlements are a physical manifestation of the values of its inhabitants (*Law 1*), this means, by extension, that those who move also bring along building practices that embody those values. This tendency is evident in many studies of migration patterns of vernacular architecture across vast distances. Several excellent books by Paul Oliver serve as strong resources around this subject.

As one of the more recent mass migrations, research tracking the movement of vernacular and folk architecture across North America is particularly telling: showing how building types were brought from overseas and adapted as they swept across the New World, in response to a variety of forces including geography, technologies available and local materials (*Laws 26-27* and *Laws 30-32*). This process is captured by Virginia and Lee McAlester in their comprehensive *A Field Guide to American Houses* describing how "European colonists…imported their own building techniques, but adapted these to local materials used by the Natives—wood in the heavily forested eastern half of the country and stone or clay in the more arid West."

Henry Glassie describes the process more poetically: "When the builder's attention is narrowed by training, whether in the dusty shop of a master carpenter or the sleek classroom of a university, past experience is not obliterated. It endures in the strange caves of the brain and in old habits of the muscles as they seek smooth routes through the air. Education adds a layer. In precept and admonition, in pedagogical technique if not in content, the teacher brings cultural values into the process of transmission. Students obey or rebel. Inwardly, new ideas mix and coexist with old ones, and the mind, fed by the senses, continues to bounce about, unfettered by consistency. Resolution will come in performance, in dedicated, situated instants of concentration, while planning meets accidents and learning continues."

REFERENCES:
- **Constantino Doxiadis** - *Ekistics: The Science of Human Settlements*
- **Henri Pirenne** - *Medieval Cities: Their Origins and the Revival of Trade*
- **Paul Oliver** - *Dwellings: The Vernacular House World Wide*
- **Paul Oliver** - *Encyclopedia of Vernacular Architecture of the World*
- **Paul Oliver, Marcel Vellinga, Alexander Bridge** - *Encyclopedia of Vernacular Architecture of the World*
- **Virginia and Lee McAlester** - *A Field Guide to American Houses*
- **Henry Glassie** - *Material Culture*

16. The death process of all or part of a settlement will not occur until its initial value has been amortized from the economic and cultural points of view.

Barring exceptional circumstances, investment in a settlement, or piece of it, will not be eliminated until the time taken for it to be paid off. That is, according to Doxiadis, it will not be allowed to decline until it has been amortized in full. Given the current rate of construction and global change, examples of decline occurring before amortization are more frequent than in the past but, relatively speaking, the examples remain rare.

So, for example, if a shopping mall is built is for a particular neighbourhood and requires a 50-year amortization period, it will not typically fall into ruin prior to that time. This being the case, built environments are particularly vulnerable to decline after the period of amortization has expired. It is here that maintenance and (re)creation become

GRANADA, SPAIN

critical for its future existence (*Law 5*). In the absence of the latter, a settlement will tend towards death.

North American shopping malls are an interesting example. With the first wave of malls built in the 1950s and fully amortized just prior to the turn of the century, the past two decades have seen the death and/or transformation of many of the original structures. As recently as 2016, retail analyst Jan Kniffen predicted that "about 400 of the country's 1,100 enclosed malls will fail in the upcoming years." Of those that remain, he stated that about 250 will thrive and the rest will continue to struggle. According to him, this has happened in response to the growth of online shopping and different consumer preferences. With 2,000 regional malls in existence just a decade before Kniffen's prediction, the steady decline has been ongoing. The births of mall variants, such as "Lifestyle Centres," have resulted.

A rare instance of what happens when a project falls into decline prior to amortization is the 45-story tower in Caracas—Torre David—that was abandoned due to the death of its developer in 1993 and the '94 collapse of the Venezuelan economy. Here, 'slum families' occupied the building, and it became the container of several 'informal vertical communities,' with hundreds of people. This process is thoroughly described in *Torre David: Informal Vertical Communities*.

REFERENCES:
- **Constantino Doxiadis** - *Ekistics: The Science of Human Settlements*
- **Kerry Close - "A Third of American Malls Will Close Soon"** - *http://time.com/money/4327632/shopping-malls-closing/*

- Koolhaas, *GSD Project on the City - Guide to Shopping*
- Alfredo Brillembourg (Editor), Hubert Klumpner (Editor), Urban-Think Tank (Editor), ETH Zurich - *Torre David: Informal Vertical Communities*

17. **In the death process of a settlement, its elements do not die simultaneously. The same holds true for the values that it represents. As a consequence, the settlement as a whole has much greater chances of surviving and developing through renewal, even if some of its elements are dying.**

Law 5 introduced the idea that different physical elements of a human settlement last for different lengths of time. This was captured through the work of those such as Stewart Brand. Twenty-six years prior to Brand's *How Buildings Learn*, however, Doxiadis highlighted this same idea, naming five specific elements—Nature, Man, Society, Shells, and Networks. Through these elements, individually or in combination, he believed a settlement had the opportunity to regenerate or continue living, if in decline. Regardless of the specific categories, it is critical to note that the elements are scalar in nature (*Law 0*) and that the life-cycle of different elements plays a potential role in potentially elongating the life of a human settlement.

Henri Pirenne's research tracking the transformation of medieval cities across the fall of the Roman Empire demonstrates, for example, how certain aspects of the physical fabric—buildings, infrastructure, etc.—endured over time. Similarly, Anthony Morris' exhaustive study of urban form before the industrial revolution describes many

CHAPTER 1: Laws of Development - Extinction

BARCELONA, SPAIN

similar instances, with the urban fabric of ancient Rome being an iconic example of how the urban structure and buildings served as the basis of the "decline, fall, and eventual resurgence of the city."

Adding to this idea, however, Doxiadis also highlights softer aspects of settlement life—economic, social, political, technical and cultural/aesthetic—as having similar differences in lifespan. The continued use of architectural elements from ancient civilizations (such as the Ancient Greek Orders) can be seen as a connection to past socio-cultural values that these earlier elements embodied. Similarly, much evidence clearly speaks to how the economic practices of the Roman Empire outlived its official life (Pirenne).

These examples speak to the various aspects of a settlement—hard and soft—that carry with them different potential survival times. This remains important to understanding the overall life-cycle of human settlements.

REFERENCES:
- **Constantino Doxiadis** - *Ekistics: The Science of Human Settlements*
- **Stewart Brand** - *How Building Learn: What Happens After They're Built*
- **Henri Pirenne** - *Medieval Cities: Their Origins and the Revival of Trade*
- **Anthony E.J. Morris** - *History of Urban Form: Before the Industrial Revolution*

18. During the process of death, inertia caused by existing forces, especially buildings, plays a very important role in slowing down— or even reversing—the process.

Elaborating on *Law 17*, this law highlights the importance of built structures—what Doxiadis calls "Shells"—in slowing down the process of death of a human settlement. Simply put, the nature of the buildings in a settlement determines the strength of inertia of a built environment.

This being the case, structures that have the capacity to survive long periods of time extend the possibility of finding new life in the future, even if they have been abandoned. This process is blatantly evident across the many old settlements around the world that went into decline and have since found new life.

However, more contemporary counterparts are also plentiful, such as the former gold-mining town of Walhalla, Australia—east of Melbourne. This settlement fell into disuse after the closing of its mining operation in 1914 and has since had a small renaissance as a holiday destination and tourist hub. Given the nature of human settlements, this same process can occur at a variety of scales (*Law 0*) and many city dwellers have witnessed this at the neighbourhood level. Berlin and Detroit stand out as strong contemporary examples.

Perhaps nobody summarized the possibilities of this law more eloquently than Jane Jacobs: "Cities need old buildings so badly it is probably impossible for vigorous streets and districts to grow without them....for really new ideas of any kind--no matter how ultimately profitable or otherwise successful some of them might prove to be--there is no leeway for such chancy trial, error and experimentation in the high-overhead economy of new construction. Old ideas can sometimes use new buildings. New ideas must use old buildings."

One should be mindful, however, that there is constant tension between social pressures and the built world. Anne Vernez Moudon states: "A perfect "fit," however, between material space and social space is necessarily of short duration; material space, once built, is difficult to modify quickly, while activities and specific social needs change rapidly."

It is also important to note that although this law may seem to support the desire for immortality through monumental architecture, the history of settlements is filled with many more examples of even the strongest materials having no power against the inevitable and continuous blows of time and change.

Furthermore, factors outside the physical—social, political, economic, cultural, etc. (*Law 5*)—are also powerful agents of inertia and can contribute to, or counteract, the transformation of settlements (*Law 17*). This can be for good or ill. NIMBYism, characterized by residents opposing new development, is a popular example of the socio-cultural factors that support settlement inertia.

REFERENCES:
- **Constantino Doxiadis** - *Ekistics: The Science of Human Settlements*
- **Henri Pirenne** - *Medieval Cities: Their Origins and the Revival of Trade*
- **John Aldersea and Barbara Hood** - *Walhalla, Valley of Gold: a Story of Its People, Places and Its Gold Mines*

- Ricky Burdett (Editor) and Deyan Sudjic (Editor) - *The Endless City: The Urban Age Project* **by the London School of Economics and Deutsche Bank's Alfred Herrhausen Society,**
- Jane Jacobs - *The Death and Life of Great American Cities*
- Serge Salat - *Cities and Forms: On Sustainable Urbanism*
- Anne Vernez Moudon - *Built for Change: Neighbourhood Architecture in San Francisco*
- Paul Shepherd - *Buildings: Between Living Time and Rocky Space*

19. The death process of a settlement is complete when every reason for its life has ceased to exist and/or when the needs it fulfilled within its larger system can be provided elsewhere to a better degree and/or with easier access.

Given that settlements are products of different forces and pressures coming together to satisfy human needs—physical or otherwise (*Law 1-5*)—the process of death is complete when all the functions it provides within the larger system of settlements (*Law 0*) have been exhausted. Built structures can potentially slow down the death process and provide a framework for revival (*Law 18*), but even this has a potential time limit. Well-known examples from around the globe are many, from Machu Picchu in Peru and Çatalhöyük, Turkey to Skara Brae, Scotland and Memphis in Egypt. Although certain building elements remain, in the absence of inhabitants the settlement has effectively died.

Reasons for their demise are many, but barring the rare instances where the needs these settlements satisfy go obsolete in and of themselves, the

SACRED VALLEY, PERU

death process often occurs when the functions are provided more effectively by another (nearby) settlement. At a small scale, this process can be seen in the decline of the America "High Street" by regional shopping malls between the 1950s and 1970s. This is well described in the works of Miles Orvell, James Howard Kunstler, and John Stilgoe, who demonstrated how easier access (via automobiles) and a wide array of centralized services caused the shift from street to mall. As illustrated in *Law 16*, a similar process is now affecting the death, demolition, or transformation of these same shopping malls.

REFERENCES:
- **Constantino Doxiadis** - *Ekistics: The Science of Human Settlements*
- **Rem Koolhaas** - *GSD Project on the City II- Guide to Shopping*
- **Miles Orvell** - *The Death and Life of Main Street: Small Towns in American Memory, Space, and Community*
- **James Howard Kunstler** - *The Geography of Nowhere*
- **John Stilgoe** - *Outside Lies Magic*

20. The creation, development and death of settlements follow certain laws unless humans decide otherwise.

The implications behind this law are more complex than they seem. Doxiadis simply explains the principle with one sentence: "The question whether he is able or wants to is one depending to a great extent on the laws themselves."

This seemingly straightforward phrase puts forth the idea that humans have a choice in determining the directions of their settlements. This is certainly true, but only to a certain extent. People, for example, can 'choose' to let a development die prior to full amortization, but in the face of a constantly uncertain future, predictions of the future conditions upon which decisions are based can be flawed.

This being the case, a lot of research has been done since Doxiadis' time around cognition and decision-making. The work of Nobel Memorial Prize in Economics laureate Daniel Kahneman in *Thinking, Fast and Slow* is particularly relevant. Within the book, Kahneman summarizes extensive research around different modes of thought, cognitive biases and errors in human judgment that become particularly acute when faced with complex scenarios, such as planning human settlements.

Unfortunately, describing his findings are beyond the scope of this short entry, but it finds parallels in Jared Diamond's *Collapse* that focuses on how "societies end up destroying themselves through disastrous decisions..." Diamond's work points explicitly to the failures of individual and group decision-making when it comes to the 'collective good'.

It's quite clear then that Doxiadis' use of the word 'decide' within this law should be taken with a grain of salt. The processes by which decisions are made are as much a part of human settlements as anything else.

REFERENCES:
- **Constantino Doxiadis** - *Ekistics: The Science of Human Settlements*
- **Daniel Kahneman** - *Thinking, Fast and Slow*
- **Jared Diamond** - *Collapse*
- **Joseph Tainter** - *Collapse of Complex Societies*

PANAMA CITY, PANAMA

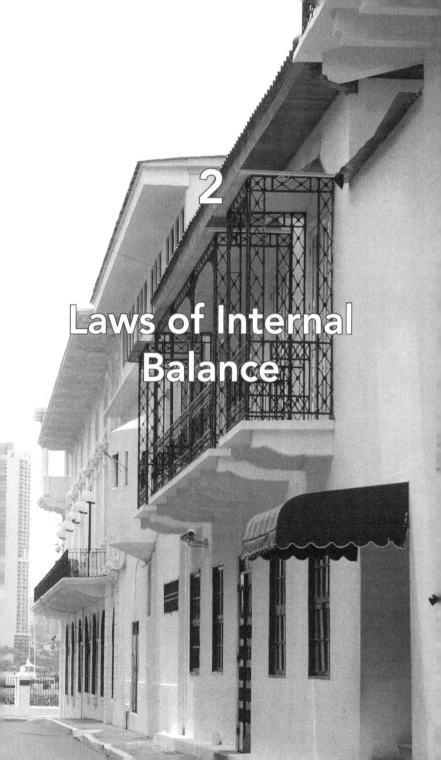

2
Laws of Internal Balance

21. The elements in each part of a settlement tend toward balance.

This combines two of Doxiadis' original laws, each of which is intimately interconnected. As noted in *Law 5*, all the elements inherent to a settlement—those cutting across physical, social, political, economic and cultural spheres of life—require being in 'balance' in order for the settlement to survive. This balance sits within a range that each settlement strives to stay within.

Doxiadis cites the example of a settlement whose rapid growth spurs the development of shelters to house the incoming population. If the creation of shelters is done within a 'reasonable' time frame, the settlement remains orderly and stable. If, on the other hand, it does not respond quickly enough to the forces exerted, instability and disorder can result. Jared Diamond described such cases in *Collapse* where societal decline resulted from an inability to effectively manage environmental resources relative to the demands of the population.

At the end of the day, a settlement only performs well when balance exists. However, the balance must exist across all scales (*Law 0*) to ultimately be effective. According to Doxiadis, those scales that do not achieve this balance will need renewal and/or development.

FURTHER READING:
- **Constantino Doxiadis** - *Ekistics: The Science of Human Settlements,*
- **Jared Diamond** - *Collapse*
- **Joseph Tainter** - *Collapse of Complex Societies*

22. The balance among the elements of a settlement is dynamic balance.

Building on the fact that development of a settlement is a continuous process (*Law 7*), the balance that must be maintained between elements is dynamic in nature. A settlement must respond to the changing forces being exerted on them at any given time, towards gaining some form of balance (*Law 21*), unless it is hindered artificially.

An increasing and diversifying population, requires more differentiated housing, institutions, facilities, and functions, for example. In the absence of a more formal, 'official' means of supplying the latter, informal structures and settlements tend to develop. This process is well described by many well-known authors, such as Mike Davis and Stephen Graham.

Critical to the discussion of this principle is the idea of homeostasis—the condition that describes, "a relatively stable state of equilibrium or a tendency toward such a state between the different but interdependent elements or groups of elements of an organism, population, or group" (Merriam-Webster).

Referring to the "organic model" of settlement form—one of the three normative models put forth in *Good City Form*—Kevin Lynch describes the connection between homeostasis and settlement as developing from applying the insights in ecology and biology to the built world. Those who go by this model believe that settlements "...are born and come to maturity, like organisms. (Unlike organisms, however, they should not die) Functions are rhythmic, and the healthy community is stable

MACHU PICCHU, PERU

by virtue of maintaining its dynamic, homeostatic balance. Societies and resources are permanently conserved by this uninterrupted cycling and balancing." Lynch also offers a sharp critique of this model, within the book.

FURTHER READING:
- **Constantino Doxiadis** - *Ekistics: The Science of Human Settlements*
- **Jared Diamond** - *Collapse*
- **Joseph Tainter** - *Collapse of Complex Societies*
- **Mike Davis** - *Planet of Slums*
- **Stephen Graham** - *Vertical: The City from Satellites to Bunkers*
- **Kevin Lynch** - *Good City Form*

23. The balance of the elements is expressed in different ways in each phase of the creation and evolution of a settlement.

As with any dynamic and complex system, the elements and forces exerted on settlements vary with each stage of its development. At the early stages, for example, issues pertaining to the direct manipulation of its landscape and natural setting are paramount: cutting trees, manipulating water courses, leveling topography, to name just a few, are top priority. As time passes, buildings must be suitably built—starting out as more temporary, then often developing into more permanent fixtures. This process is ongoing.

Recent decades have seen the development of more sophisticated tools and technologies of design, construction and destruction. These, in turn, have changed the rate at which development occurs.

As a result, the phases of settlement seem to have quickened, with some cities being built seemingly overnight. Thomas J. Campanella's *The Concrete Dragon*, thoroughly describes this process in China. As does Rem Koolhaas' *GSD Project on the City II - Great Leap Forward*.

Regardless of speed, however, human settlements continue to evolve as new elements and forces in need of continuous stabilization are exerted on it.

FURTHER READING:
- **Constantino Doxiadis** - *Ekistics: The Science of Human Settlements*
- **Thomas J. Campanella** - *The Concrete Dragon: China's Urban Revolution and What it Means for the World*

24. The balance between the elements is expressed differently at each scale of a settlement, while each scale interacts dynamically with others.

Settlements are in a constant state of dynamic change, continuously adapted by its inhabitants in response to the forces being exerted upon it (*Law 22*). As described in *Law 21* and *23*, settlements also tend towards achieving equilibrium across interacting scales (Law 0). As such, balance is expressed differently across scales.

Thus, if balance is to be achieved at a scale that is controlled at the individual level—say, the scale of a room or house—it would be expressed very differently than one where larger groups of people are involved—such as highway traffic.

Making things more complex, the forces exerted on settlements that must find resolution often cut across interacting scales. Transportation is particularly relevant to this issue since it touches a variety of scales across time, speed and distance—from walking down the street to regional access. This in turn has very physical and tangible effects on issues such as street widths and public realm design. Jarrett Walker's wonderfully accessible book, *Human Transit*, speaks well to this issue of balance and scalar solutions related to public transit.

This idea also forms the basis of many important books and ideas—including Christopher Alexander, Ian McHarg, Jane Jacobs and Renee Chow to N.J. Habraken, Jan Gehl, Edmund Bacon, and Wenche Dramstad—each of which adds a voice around problems and solutions to human settlement at different scales. In real terms, one can strongly argue that this law exemplifies the ultimate problem of settlements: balancing solutions unique to specific scales with a keen understanding of how they will affect the greater system.

FURTHER READING:
- **Constantino Doxiadis** - *Ekistics: The Science of Human Settlements*
- **Jarrett Walker** - *Human Transit: How Clearer Thinking about Public Transit Can Enrich Our Communities and Our Lives*
- **Christopher Alexander** - *A Pattern Language*
- **Ian McHarg** - *Design With Nature*
- **Jane Jacobs** - *The Death and Life of Great American Cities*
- **Renee Chow** - *Suburban Space*
- **N.J. Habraken** - *Structure of The Ordinary*
- **Jan Gehl** - *Cities for People*
- **Edmond Bacon** - *Design of Cities*
- **Dramstad/Olson,/Forman** - *Landscape Ecology Principles in Landscape Architecture and Land-Use Planning*

25. Across all scales of settlement, achieving balance within the range of the human scale is critically important for its long-term success. This scale corresponds to the extents of ones control, as well as the body and senses— roughly a ten minute walking distance.

In the wake of the growing popularity of Transit-Oriented Development, the significance of the ten-minute walking distance has become very well known. So, perhaps it may come as a surprise to many that Doxiadis stated it almost half a century ago. It is worth noting that I slightly altered this law, as Doxiadis elevated the human scale as the most important scale within which to achieve balance. But in light of the many contemporary settlements that have thrived despite a blatant disregard to "the human scale", I chose to lower its importance slightly.

After decades of neglect, the human scale has risen as one of the most significant motivations behind transforming settlements, however. So, one could argue that Doxiadis' original sentiments on the issue are the more accurate. This is clearly exemplified by increased interest in Transit-Oriented Development, mentioned above, as well as the popularity of the writings that speak to this.

Among the most common are the books of Jan Gehl. Building from the seminal research of anthropologist Edward T. Hall and his concept of proxemics in the 1960s (studying the use of space and its effect on humans) Gehl's insights into the human senses and its implications on the design of cities have become an anchor for best design practices around the world. These are used specifically towards creating pedestrian-oriented environments.

CHAPTER 2: Laws of Internal Balance 93

GRANADA, SPAIN

This being the case, the (homeostatic) argument that settlements tend toward equilibrium around human scale and experience is still on the table (*Law 22*). If not the most important variable with respect to human settlements, current experience shows that it remains critical to its long-term well being.

It's also worth noting that discussions around walking distances have diversified since its early days, as well. Initially, walking distances were measured simply 'as the crow flies' but more recent endeavours have also included the impact of street geometries and land-use, among other attributes. In *Happy City*, for example, Charles Montgomery compares a ten-minute walking radius within two different contexts—the gridded Midtown, Atlanta and a suburban counterpart, Mableton, composed of a dendritic pattern of cul-de-sacs. The research showed that the influence of street geometries and land-use patterns greatly influences the behaviour of residents. In his words, and in keeping with the observations of Jane Jacobs: "Connectivity counts: more intersections mean more walking, and more disconnected cul-de-sacs mean more driving."

Furthermore, culture also matters. In *A Geography Of Time: On Tempo, Culture, And The Pace Of Life*, for example, social psychologist Robert V. Levine highlights how one's sense of time is greatly influenced by culture, extending to the pace of a person's gait.

FURTHER READING:
- **Constantino Doxiadis** - *Ekistics: The Science of Human Settlements*
- **Peter Calthorpe** - *The Next American Metropolis: Ecology, Community, and the American Dream*,

- **Hank Dittmar and Gloria Ohland** - *The New Transit Town: Best Practices In Transit-Oriented Development*
- **Jan Gehl** - *Life Between Buildings* and *Cities for People*
- **Edward T. Hall** - *The Hidden Dimension*
- **Charles Montgomery** - *Happy City: Transforming Our Live Through Urban Design*
- **Jane Jacobs** - *The Death and Life of Great American Cities*
- **Robert V. Levine** - *A Geography Of Time: On Tempo, Culture, And The Pace Of Life*

GUADIX, SPAIN

3
Laws of Physical Characteristics

LOCATION

26. The geographic/topographic location of a settlement depends on the needs it must serve for itself (its inhabitants, natural setting, etc.) and the larger co-dependent settlement system to which it belongs.

Geography has played a dominant role in the creation of settlements since their beginning. That the choice of physical location and natural setting depends on the needs of its inhabitants is clear. Settlements founded on water-based trade and/or industry are located on or near water bodies, for example, while resource towns must be near their specific resource. But this also depends on their role and position within the larger co-dependent system (*Law 0*). This is apparent in the construction and distribution of Roman settlements around the Mediterranean rim and across Europe, where strategic geographic positions were chosen, leveraging their natural setting and greater role within the Empire (military, trade, etc.).

Jack Williams' wonderful examination of small towns along the Appalachian Mountains of the United States in *East 40 Degrees: An Interpretive Atlas* clearly demonstrates this law in action within the past three centuries, across various settlements between Alabama and Maine. He even ultimately describes their urban forms typologically, in relation to their role and natural settings. "River Town", "Railroad Town", "Coal Town", and "Coastal Town" are a few of the names given.

CHAPTER 3: Laws of Physical Characteristics - Location

GRANADA, SPAIN

Although our ability and willingness to manipulate natural settings to make human settlements has increased aggressively and the 'roles' played by settlements within our global system has increased in complexity, this law is no less true for the settlements being built today. Geographic opportunities and constraints, in tandem with strategic roles (political, commercial, etc.) continue to dictate contemporary building practices.

Interestingly, and as outlined in *Laws 17-18*, the inertia of settlements allows for changing values towards geography, nature and role within the larger system to ebb and flow, as they are (re)interpreted by different societies over time (*Law 1*). This is the case for many of the industrial cities that grew from prior settlements with key geographic locations accessing distribution networks, such as Dusseldorf and Detroit. This process, in fact, characterizes the nature of many settlements that survive over the long-term, as Henri Pirenne's seminal work describing the decline and rebirth of Roman settlements across the Middle Ages demonstrates.

FURTHER READING:
- **Constantino Doxiadis** - *Ekistics: The Science of Human Settlements*
- **Jack Williams** - *East 40 Degrees: An Interpretive Atlas*
- **Paul Knox** - *Atlas of Cities*
- **Spiro Kostof** - *The City Shaped*
- **Jared Diamond** - *Guns Germs and Steel* and *Collapse*
- **Henri Pirenne** - *Medieval Cities: Their Origins and the Revival of Trade*

27. The geographic/topographic location of a settlement depends on its needs, geology, anticipated physical size and technology available.

Elaborating on *Law 26*, this law introduces issues of the anticipated physical limits of a settlement and the influence of geography and topography. Given that the boundaries of a settlement are directly related to geology (soil conditions, etc.) as well as the technologies available to the society, these have been added to Doxiadis' original law.

The simplicity of this law masks a more complex underbelly. Logically, those choosing a site for a settlement would look to geographic and topographic constraints, and weigh these against their longer-term vision for the settlement (i.e. how many people they anticipate living within it). But this decision is clearly based on various assumptions and speculations, laden with cultural values and technological limitations that may change over time (*Law 1*).

As discussed in *Laws 1-2* and *4-6*, the 'needs' of inhabitants are varied and elaborate. So, we encounter the construction of settlements for a variety of reasons, in locations that may seem outright illogical when viewed by different cultures.

The 15th century mountaintop community of Machu Picchu is a case in point. Nestled between two peaks along the crest of a mountain range, it is difficult for most to understand why a society would put such effort towards the creation of a settlement so difficult to access. Yet, it met the 'needs' of its inhabitants. Describing the creation of cities based on a cosmic model (versus those models focused on 'efficiency' and/or the 'organic') the now retired MIT Professor Julian Bienart stated: "It is only for the gods that man exerts himself." Machu Picchu might be grouped within this category, alongside others such as Angkor Wat (Cambodia), Teotihuacán (Mexico) and Çatalhöyük (Turkey).

The impact of technology (and geology) on a settlement's physical size is also critical. This is apparent in the transformation of the favelas of Rio. Although the 'natural' and 'official' city boundaries are prescribed by stable terrain on the lower fringes of the surrounding mountains, various pressures have created informal settlements that cling to the steep, geologically unstable slopes of these towering ranges.

Over time, with changing technologies and growing wealth, however, these slopes are being stabilized and redeveloped by the wealthy in light of the views they provide over the city. In effect, Rio's natural and official city limits are effectively being 'redrawn' in response to changing values and technologies—a process succinctly described in Stephen Graham's *Vertical: The City from Satellites to Bunkers*.

FURTHER READING:
- **Constantino Doxiadis** - *Ekistics: The Science of Human Settlements*
- **MIT course Theory of City Form - Julian Bienart - Lecture 2:** *Normative Theory I: The City as Supernatural*
  - https://ocw.mit.edu/courses/architecture/4-241j-theory-of-city-form-spring-2013/video-lectures/lec-2-normative-theory-i-the-city-as-supernatural/
- **Stephen Graham** - *Vertical: The City from Satellites to Bunkers*

CHAPTER 3: Laws of Physical Characteristics - Location

PARIS, FRANCE

METRO VANCOUVER, CANADA

SIZE

28. The population size of a settlement depends on its roles in serving certain needs for its inhabitant and for its larger settlement system.

Issues around optimal population size and settlements have a long history, stretching back to Aristotle. Many intelligent voices have spoken their opinions on the matter, including Leonardo and Ebenezer Howard, founder of the Garden City Movement. Milton Keynes in Buckinghamshire, England, a settlement greatly influenced by Howard, was designed for a target of 250,000 in the 1960s, for example. More recently, The Pragmatist's Pavel Podolyak put forth his opinion suggesting: "optimum national sizes to be 10-50 million, optimum city size of 1 million and below for most major cities in a country, and the exception for largest national city at no more than 5 million."

Through his extensive research, it was evident to Doxiadis that settlements came in a very wide range of shapes and sizes, with an equally diverse population base. As such, classification of any sort would be "somewhat arbitrary." However, he also recognized that their diversity required a classification system in order to allow study. So, he offered his own scalar classification system—the *Ekistic Logarithmic Scale*—arranging a series of fifteen scalar units (*Law 0*) according to population and area.

Without delving into the specifics of Doxiadis' system, it is important to note that he considered the smallest 'unit' of settlement the human being. At the opposite extreme lay the *Ecumenopolis*, a planet-wide settlement system of over 30,000,000,000 people that still respected human dimensions (*Law 25*).

In contrast to many who have put forth exact estimates on optimal size, Doxiadis believed that there was neither a specific number that defined the ideal population size, nor necessarily any limits. To his mind, settlements could—and should—grow in line with the needs of the inhabitants and its (dynamic) role within its larger settlement system.

The iconic image of NASA's *View of the World at Night* speaks well to Doxiadis' prediction—showing the far-reaching interconnected global system of settlements that comprise the contemporary world.

FURTHER READING:
- **Constantino Doxiadis** - *Ekistics: The Science of Human Settlements*
- **Constantino Doxiadis et al.** - *Ecumenopolis: The inevitable city of the future*
- **Ebenezer Howard** - *Garden Cities of Tomorrow*
- **The Pragmatist (Pavel Podolyak)** - *Optimum City Population Size* - http://pavelpodolyak.blogspot.ca/2014/11/optimum-city-population-size.html
- **MIT course** - **Theory of City Form** - **Julian Bienart** - **Lecture 4:** *Normative Theory 4: The City as Organism* - https://ocw.mit.edu/courses/architecture/4-241j-theory-of-city-form-spring-2013/video-lectures/lec-4-normative-theory-iii-the-city-as-organism/
- **NASA** - *Views of the World at Night* - https://www.nasa.gov/mission_pages/NPP/news/earth-at-night.html

108 CHAPTER 3: Laws of Physical Characteristics - Size

SEVILLE, SPAIN

29. The physical size of a settlement depends on its population size, its needs, culture (technology, etc.), its role within the larger settlement system, and its geographic, topographic, climatic, and geologic conditions.

Although Doxiadis deemed population size, the needs of inhabitants, and the role within the larger settlement system as critical to a settlement's physical size, he importantly noted that material boundaries are also greatly affected by physical conditions. The original law cites only "topographic conditions", but it is critical to expand this to include geographic, climatic, and geologic circumstances. Similarly, culture (i.e. technology, values, etc.) also greatly influences the form and development patterns of settlements. Issues around the influence of technology on physical boundaries have also been described in *Law 27* with reference to the phenomenon of the favelas of Rio and their transformations.

Needless to say, the physical size and boundaries of a settlement occur at the complex convergence of all these influences. Although not speaking directly to the physical size of settlements, Amos Rapoport's *House Form and Culture* and Bernard Rudofsky's *Architecture Without Architects: A Short Introduction to Non-Pedigreed Architecture* are some of the well-known books on how culture (technology, etc.), behaviour, and the natural environment (climate, geography, etc.) influence the built world. Also worth mentioning is the work of Mark DeKay and G. Z. Brown, *Sun, Wind, and Light: Architectural Design Strategies*, that accurately speaks to how complex climatic phenomena can influence the design of settlements at various scales.

It is interesting to note that the phenomenon of settlements in decline is not included in Doxiadis' original description. Yet, given that settlements are dynamic in nature (*Law 7* and *22*), their physical size is changing continuously. Within this context, shrinking settlements are also critical to understand within the context of physical size. The German Federal Cultural Foundation's *Shrinking Cities Project* offer important resources in this area, covering cities such as Detroit and Manchester, both of which are former industrial city superpowers.

FURTHER READING:
- **Constantino Doxiadis** - *Ekistics: The Science of Human Settlements*
- **Stephen Graham** - *Vertical: The City from Satellites to Bunkers*
- **Mark DeKay and G. Z. Brown** - *Sun, Wind, and Light: Architectural Design Strategies*
- **Amos Rapoport** -*House Form and Culture*
- **Bernard Rudofsky** - *Architecture Without Architects: A Short Introduction to Non-Pedigreed Architecture*
- **Shrinking Cities** - *http://www.shrinkingcities.com/kultur_schrumpfen.0.html?&L=1*
- **McKinsey Global Institute - "Shrinking cities: the rise and fall of global urban populations – mapped" in The Guardian, Nov. 2016.** - *https://www.theguardian.com/cities/gallery/2016/nov/02/global-population-decline-cities-mapped*
- **McKinsley Global Institute, 2016, Urban world: Meeting the demographic challenge** - *file:///Users/e_vill1/Desktop/McKinsleyGlobalInstitute_Urban-World-Demographic-Challenge_Full-report.pdf*

CHAPTER 3: Laws of Physical Characteristics - Size 111

SINGAPORE

KINDERDIJK, NETHERLANDS

FUNCTIONS

30. The functions of a settlement depend on the geographic and topographic location, geologic conditions, technological development, population size, and the role within the larger settlement system.

Given the many elements presented in this law, it is worth dissecting them further to understand how they relate and expand on Doxiadis' initial insights. This is particularly important since I have added geologic and technological factors to his initial statement.

In keeping with *Law 26*, geography, topography and geology play critical roles in determining the functions of a settlement. The creation of an agricultural community, for example, is clearly dependent on those three conditions to facilitate the growth of food. Referring to Neolithic settlement in Mesopotamia, James Breasted describes how they began "….in small oases on steppes and plateaux. Despite the threat of drought the difficulties of taming soil were less formidable there than in the flood plains of major rivers."

Expanding Breasted's thoughts, Anthony Morris describes how early farming communities established themselves on higher ground over thousands of years, and gradually moved "down the valleys of the Tigris and Euphrates as the alluvial deposits dried out and as techniques, especially irrigation, were improved." This passage also highlights the importance of technologies

CHAPTER 3: Laws of Physical Characteristics - Functions

and techniques with respect to the function of a settlement.

In terms of population size, Doxiadis highlights that functions determine population size, and not the other way around. Given a settlement's dynamic nature (*Law 22*), as it develops it acquires different functions due to its size (*Law 2* and *Law 11*). As such, its functions are in constant flux.

The functions of a settlement are also conditioned by the role within the larger co-dependent settlement system (*Law 0* and *Law 8*). In the contemporary world of global trade and technological innovation, the intersection between all the factors within this law has shown a number of interesting results. The development of Memphis, Tennessee as the home of the Federal Express cargo airline global "SuperHub" due to its geographic location is a case in point. Issues around roles are elaborated on further in *Law 31*.

It is worth noting, however, that discussions around the role and function of a settlement must necessarily engage the issue of time (*Law 14*).

FURTHER READING:
- **Constantino Doxiadis** - *Ekistics: The Science of Human Settlements*
- **James Henry Breasted** - *Ancient times, A History of the Early World: An Introduction to the study of Ancient History and the Career of Early Man*
- **Anthony E.J. Morris** - *History of Urban Form Before the Industrial Revolution*

31. The role of a settlement within its larger co-dependent system depends on its function, geographic/topographic location and population size.

Intimately related to *Laws 26-27*, the role of a settlement within its larger co-dependent system depends significantly on its geographic location. According to Doxiadis, the latter governs its class. However, its function also plays a part in this relationship.

As noted in *Law 30*, time is a very important variable in this equation, as functions and role can change based on different cultural values and technological advances. The example of Memphis, Tennessee as the Federal Express global "Superhub" was already given in *Law 30*, but there are many more examples, big and small.

Population size dynamically responds to the changing functions and adds to, or detracts from, its role within the larger co-dependent system. Doxiadis suggests that this results in, "changing and reclassifying the settlement within the whole system." These changes can increase or decrease the importance of the settlement within the system.

The unpredicted popularity of Squamish, British Columbia as a contemporary global kiteboarding hotspot and growing recreation node is an interesting example. Its location within driving distance of Vancouver—itself an international draw—at the head of the Squamish River Delta where land, mountains and water converge to create strong winds through the Howe Sound fjord, have contributed to its increasing role and consequent growth.

FURTHER READING:
- **Constantino Doxiadis** - *Ekistics: The Science of Human Settlements*
- **Anthony E.J. Morris** - *History of Urban Form Before the Industrial Revolution*
- **John Clague and Bob Turner** - *Vancouver, City on the Edge: Living with a Dynamic Geological Landscape*

32. The functions and role of a settlement are interdependent with geography, topographic conditions, geological circumstance, as well as population and physical size.

As implied in *Law 30* and *Law 31*, this law formally states that geographic location, topographic circumstances, as well as population and physical size are interdependent. Doxiadis is explicit in the fact that, despite the latter, a hierarchy exists between these factors, with greater value placed on certain relationships than others. This is the reason why the previous two laws (*Laws 30* and *31*) place emphasis in certain directions.

This law, specifically, is meant to summarize the relationships between all the factors cited in *Laws 26-31*. The diagram following this law, shows how geographic location, topographic conditions, "Ekistic role" (within the larger settlement system), population size and physical size "form a circle within which all possible connections are justified to different degrees. There are no missing links between the circles; some of them are simply stronger than others. The radiation of these circles represents one of the previous six laws while the total stands for the law of interdependence."

We must also remember the importance of technological development, however. As discussed several times within the *Laws 30* and *31*, it has a strong relationship to people's world view and relationship to the natural and physical worlds.

FURTHER READING:
- **Constantino Doxiadis** - *Ekistics: The Science of Human Settlements*
- **Anthony E.J. Morris** - *History of Urban Form Before the Industrial Revolution*
- **James Henry Breasted** - *Ancient times, A History of the Early World: An Introduction to the study of Ancient History and the Career of Early Man*
- **Peter Hall** - *Cities in Civilization*
- **Ian McHarg** - *Design With Nature*
- **Henri Pirenne** - *Medieval Cities: Their Origins and the Revival of Trade*
- **Amos Rapoport** - *House Form and Culture*
- **Bernard Rudofsky** - *Architecture Without Architects: A Short Introduction to Non-Pedigreed Architecture*

CHAPTER 3: Laws of Physical Characteristics - Functions

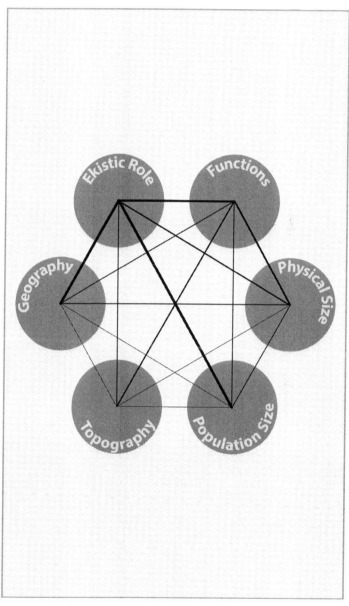

DOXIADIS' INTERDEPENDENCE OF FACTORS AND FUNCTIONS (LAW 32)

PARIS, FRANCE

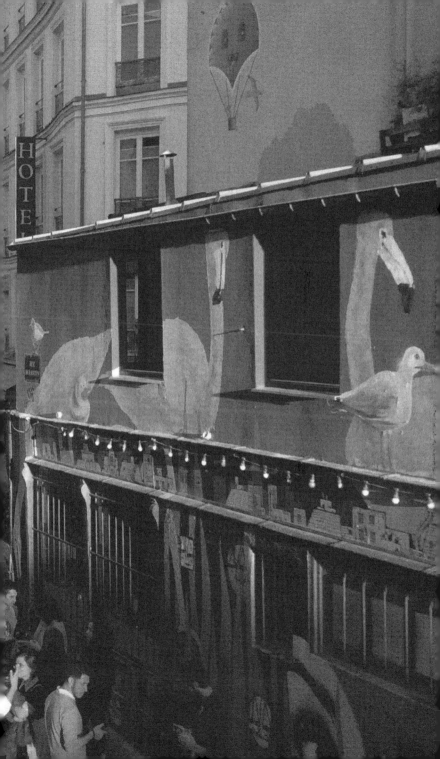

STRUCTURE

33. The basic cell of human settlement is a physical scalar unit that is an expression of its community—politically, socially, culturally, economically, etc. The settlement will only function properly only if this unit is not fragmented in any way.

Law 1 states that the physical fabric of a settlement is an expression of a community's values—political, social, economic, cultural, etc. The material manifestations of these dimensions are critical to its well-being and established at a series of different scales (*Law 0* and *Law 8*). However, some are more important to their respective communities than others and unique to each settlement.

Ray Oldenburg echoed this thirty years later in his influential book *The Great Good Place*. Within, he describes the importance of the "third place"—inclusive social places separate from home and work—and their roles in developing a healthy community. His work cites a number of historical examples, from the French Cafe to the American Main Street, that have served this purpose over time. As one can see, they are different and range in scale, and Oldenburg suggests that they served as critical "informal public gathering places" that unified neighbourhoods, among other important social functions.

Similarly, in *Built for Change*, Anne Vernez Moudon cites the 'Building/House' as the basic cell of the city, while the lot acted as the "basic cell of neighbourhood". She goes on further to discuss how tenure and inhabitation act as ways of controlling the residential cell.

Whatever the scale, Doxiadis states that these important physical places must remain intact in order for communities within a settlement to function properly. .

FURTHER READING:
- **Constantino Doxiadis** - *Ekistics: The Science of Human Settlements*
- **Ray Oldenburg** - *The Great Good Place* and "**Our Vanishing 'Third Places**" http://plannersweb.com/wp-content/uploads/1997/01/184.pdf
- **Anne Vernez Moudon** - *Built for Change: Neighbourhood Architecture in San Francisco*

34. All communities, and therefore, all settlement scalar units tend to be connected to each other hierarchically. Every community of a higher order serves a certain number of communities of a lower order, and the same is true of specific functions with each unit.

Although the physical scalar units that comprise a settlement are co-dependent (*Law 8*), the relationship between these elements has not been discussed until now. This law establishes a hierarchical structure connecting units within a larger system. This is in keeping with some of the pioneering work around hierarchy theory at that time, such as Arthur Koestler' s *The Ghost in the Machine* (1967) and Lancelot Law Whyte, Albert G. Wilson, and Donna Wilson (Editors) - *Hierarchical structures* (1969).

CHAPTER 3: Laws of Physical Characteristics - Structure

GRANADA, SPAIN

Since the release of *Ekistics*, advances in knowledge around ecological systems, complexity theory and hierarchy theory have been more definitively applied to biological structures, as well as cities. These have served to substantiate Doxiadis' claims.

With respect to urban structure, nested hierarchies have been a particular focus. Nikos Salingaros, for example, cites *Hierarchy* as one of the eight interconnected rules or "generic principles" of urban form. He states that *Hierarchy* links many distinct elements at specific scales interdependently (another one of his rules): that is, the relationship is not symmetrical (*Law 35*).

Salingaros is in good company, from Spiro Kostof who describes cities as "....locked in an urban system, and urban hierarchy" to N.J. Habraken who opens the discussion up to a variety of hierarchies related to settlement. These include, but are not limited to, hierarchies of circulation networks, enclosure, inclusion, and territory.

Also noteworthy is the work of Serge Salat, who suggests that, in order to create sustainable, resilient cities, three different types of hierarchies must be harmonized: "The hierarchies of built forms (urban blocks, neighbourhoods, districts, cities), the networks of communication, and the urban services connect these units on every scale and such human activities as living, working, commerce, education, and leisure from so many superimposed hierarchies."

Since this idea a little abstract, a quick example is worth describing. Consider a situation where a town acts as the main centre of a set of lower order (smaller) settlements, while simultaneously serving a larger (higher order) city. NASA's *View of the World at Night*, that clearly depicts clustered constellations of settlements, clearly shows these types of hierarchical relationships. Similarly, one could imagine a small, neighbourhood level shop existing at a "lower level" than a regional distributor from which it gets its products.

FURTHER READING:
- **Constantino Doxiadis** - *Ekistics: The Science of Human Settlements*
- **Arthur Koestler** - *The Ghost in the Machine*
- **Lancelot Law Whyte, Albert G. Wilson, and Donna Wilson (Editors)** - *Hierarchical structures*
- **Nikos A. Salingaros** - *Principles of Urban Structure*
- **Spiro Kostof** - *The City Shaped*
- **N.J. Habraken** - *Structure of The Ordinary*
- **Serge Salat**, *Cities and Forms: On Sustainable Urbanism*
- **NASA** - *Views of the World at Night* - https://www.nasa.gov/mission_pages/NPP/news/earth-at-night.html

35. The fact that all communities tend to be connected in a hierarchical manner does not mean that this connection is an exclusive one. Many other connections at the same level or at different ones are equally possible, but for organizational purposes the connection is hierarchical.

Law 34 introduced the issue of hierarchy and nested scales that connect scalar 'units' of settlements. It also presented the work of N.J. Habraken, Nikos Salingaros, and Serge Salat that speak to this concept. Doxiadis elaborates on this by recognizing that, given the complex nature of the co-dependent systems, settlements have a variety of connections "in all directions." As such, there are a number of possible relationships between elements, some of which may not be hierarchical. This gets even more intricate when secondary and other forces (*Law 11*) are considered. Despite the latter, Doxiadis states that generally speaking "any organized activity should follow a pattern of hierarchical connections."

Of particular relevance to this law is Salingaros' discussion around another one of his "generic principles of urban form," *Interdependence*. Described immediately after the principle of *Hierarchy* (*Law 34*), he suggests that elements on different scales do not depend on one another symmetrically. That is, "a higher scale requires all lower scales, but not vice versa."

Serge Salat, who builds on the insights of Salingaros, elaborates: "A successful urban web is organized by an ordered fractal hierarchy of connections at different scales. It is connected in multiple ways without being chaotic." He adds, "If a hierarchical level is missing, the web is pathological. A hierarchy is often established over the course of history." As implied in the latter, time is also a related and important factor (*Law 14*).

FURTHER READING:
- **Constantino Doxiadis** - *Ekistics: The Science of Human Settlements*
- **Nikos A. Salingaros** - *Principles of Urban Structure*
- **Spiro Kostof** - *The City Shaped*
- **N.J. Habraken** - *Structure of The Ordinary*
- **Serge Salat,** *Cities and Forms: On Sustainable Urbanism*

36. The existence or creation of communities and functions of a higher order does not necessarily mean the elimination of those of the lower one.

This law highlights a fundamental, but often misunderstood, aspect related to hierarchy. Many often assume that the creation of a 'higher-level order' ultimately means the destruction of a lower level order, but this is not always the case. The introduction of larger neighbourhood/regional supermarket, for example, does not necessarily lead to the destruction of all small markets. Although the number of lower order functions may diminish, each order has its own function relative to the scale it is a part of.

Local corner stores, therefore, serve the needs of inhabitants that cannot effectively be handled by stores or supermarkets located too far from their homes. Simply put: people can walk to them, and this prevents their elimination, despite the potentially elevated cost of products relative to larger regional retailers.

The birth of the modern supermarket is an interesting case in point, and Doxiadis highlights the fact that when they first appeared, two erred arguments arose. On one hand, advocates of the corner store and the "small scale" opposed the larger supermarkets, describing them as inhuman. On the other, those in favour of the supermarkets denounced "small" as obsolete in the face of the automobile city, seeking to eliminate them entirely.

As stated by Doxiadis, both perspectives were "equally wrong, since there is a hierarchy of functions and communities, and the hierarchical system must function as a whole if the settlement is to function satisfactorily."

Even more relevant is the idea of a street hierarchy. The advent of the highway did not see the elimination of all street types below it, although many people tried to do so with unfortunate consequences. As stated by Serge Salat, the latter "involved razing the old fabric and inordinately enlarging the urban grid to bring it in line with the major regional throughways. This was the position taken by Le Corbusier, modernism, and the new towns in Frances. We know today that this approach was a failure."

Rare circumstances of large-scale destruction aside, most settlements saw highways simply add another level to the existing types of streets.

As an advocate of the "fractal city," Nikos Salingaros' offers a more contemporary take on Doxiadis' insight: that settlements must have structural components of all sizes, across all scales, in order to remain healthy.

FURTHER READING:
- **Constantino Doxiadis** - *Ekistics: The Science of Human Settlements*
- **Serge Salat** - *Cities and Forms: On Sustainable Urbanism*
- **Michael Southworth & Eran Ben-Joseph** - *Streets and the Shaping of Towns and Cities*
- **Nikos A. Salingaros** - *Principles of Urban Structure*

37. The types of services and satisfaction provided by a settlement's scale, community and function of a higher order to those of a lower order, depend on cost-distance and time-distance.

As discussed in *Law 36*, different services and functions relate to different scales of a particular settlement. A simple comparison of the local corner store versus the larger neighbourhood/regional supermarket was described, accordingly. However, in this law, Doxiadis elaborates further by stating that cost-distance and time-distance are important factors contributing to satisfaction of the inhabitants.

The role of both of these factors have been analyzed and developed further since the publication of *Ekistics*. As described within the *Planning and Urban Design Standards*, cost-distance—as opposed to Euclidean distances measured in straight or curved paths—measures distance that "involves the least effort in moving across a surface." This has been much easier to measure with the development of Geographic Information System (GIS) softwares that readily allow these calculations.

Time-distance measures, on the other hand, look at the time required to cross certain distances. These have become particularly important for management of constructions (tunnels, bridges, etc.) as well as transit travel (i.e. transport schedules representing bus locations along transit routes).

As eloquently described by Jarrett Walker in *Human Transit*, it is worth mentioning that, although travel times are important for good transit design—and are

CHAPTER 3: Laws of Physical Characteristics - Structure

BEIJING, CHINA

often cited for proposed transit lines—the issue of frequency is equally critical.

The uses of both types of measures aside, it is clear that each continues to play an important role in shaping the distribution of activities, uses and spaces within a settlement.

FURTHER READING:
- **Constantino Doxiadis** - *Ekistics: The Science of Human Settlements*
- **American Planning Association, Frederick R. Steiner, Kent Butler** - *Planning and Urban Design Standards*
- **Vukan R. Vuchic** - *Urban Transit Systems and Technology*
- **Jarrett Walker** - *Human Transit: How Clearer Thinking about Public Transit Can Enrich Our Communities and Our Lives*

38. The overall physical texture of a human settlement depends on its scale and the smaller components of which it is composed.

This law has been revised and simplified to capture the essence of Doxiadis' initial statement, that was riddled with ambiguity. To start, in order to better understand the intent of this law, the term "physical texture" must be defined. Interestingly, Doxiadis failed to provide a specific explanation of the term within *Ekistics*. Instead, he alluded to it through explaining "textural forces" that acted on human settlements. Within his book, "physical texture" referred to the spatial relationships and distribution of physical elements across the terrain.

Although it is not described as such, the idea of physical texture is related to the idea of a settlement's "grain"—something that has a more targeted definition. Described by Kevin Lynch as one of the four basic aspects of physical form (alongside *size, density,* and *shape*), *grain* is typically divided into fine and coarse. The former refers to settlement fabrics that have smaller blocks, narrower buildings and, hence, sharper ("finer") divisions. In contrast, the latter refers to environments that have broader, larger-scale differences. Think medieval towns (fine grain) versus typical North American suburbs (coarse grain).

Given that settlements range in size—from villages to large cities—grain can only be measured across specific scales, with larger settlements being composed of neighbourhoods of varying grain, for example. As such, Doxiadis' "physical texture" of a settlement refers to the mix of fine and coarse grain elements.

With this in mind, Doxiadis suggests that a settlement's physical texture is dependent on its scale (neighbourhood, town, metropolis, etc.) as well as the smaller component (what he calls *Ekistic modulus*) from which is it logically composed. This is best described through an example: a house (the scalar unit) is composed of rooms (smaller component). So, large rooms beget large houses. Similarly, Doxiadis puts forth the idea that small cities are composed of city blocks and, if the latter is large, the texture of this city is large.

Interestingly, he also notes that the smaller component is, itself, dynamic in response to the scale of the settlement. So, if a small city grows to a large city, its city block component gets too small to define its texture, requiring a corresponding jump to groups of blocks or "superblocks".

Clearly, a certain degree of subjective judgment is required to define what constitutes the proper smaller component unit relative to the scale of settlement. This is addressed a little more in *Law 39*. However, the idea that the texture of settlement is based on the dynamic interaction of scale and smaller component units remains powerful when thinking about the structure of a built environment. It also reminds us of Anne Vernez Moudon's insights highlighted in *Law 33*: that the building/house is a basic cell of the city while the lot is basic cell of the neighbourhood.

FURTHER READING:
- **Constantino Doxiadis** - *Ekistics: The Science of Human Settlements*
- **Kevin Lynch** - "The Form of Cities", From Scientific American 190, no 4., 1954
- **Yuri Artibise** - *Urban Fabric: The Form of Cities* - http://yuriartibise.com/urban-fabric/
- **Anne Vernez Moudon** - *Built for Change: Neighbourhood Architecture in San Francisco*

39. The texture of a human settlement changes as its dimensions change.

The major contributors as to what defines the texture of a settlement—scale and its smaller component unit—were addressed in *Law 38*. But as discussed, the choice of the "smaller unit" was left open. This law addresses the latter in a more definitive way as Doxiadis describes how the house, a group of houses or city block may be a good unit for the texture of a small city. For larger cities, however, these units are too small and therefore require reconsideration. He states: "The texture of larger human settlements should change when the population of a settlement grows from say 100,000 to one million, since the settlement is unable to operate efficiently with a texture of small blocks."

He continues, describing that in order for settlements to remain healthy, they must reshape themselves accordingly, adjusting to the new conditions. The addition of new major arteries to allow for more efficient flows of people and goods through the settlement is an example of how a settlement might accommodate growth and change. According to Doxiadis, a failure to evolve and transform—via its own inertia (*Law 19*)—results in an inappropriate texture.

Anthony E.J. Morris' historical description of ancient Rome in *History of Urban Form Before the Industrial Revolution* speaks well to this issue, as he highlights the struggles inherent to the functioning of a city that was born from the growth of the small villages that coalesced into a single urban area across lower terrain. Citing challenges including increased flooding, disease and pollution, he points out that Roman planners, architects and engineers were constantly struggling to cope with the city's natural and historical context. He states: "Add to these natural problems the planning constraints that resulted from preceding generations' attempts to overcome them...and it is by no means surprising that ancient Rome, like so many large modern urban centres, was incapable of being comprehensively restructured. At best, there could only be piecemeal 'town-patching' measures."

As a counterpoint to Rome, Georges-Eugène Haussman's radical reorganization of Paris' urban fabric in the mid-19th century—widening streets and connecting monuments across the existing fine-grained city—demonstrates the accommodation of a new texture within an existing city, in response to its growth. The addition of a new scale of street and pubic space added to Paris' hierarchy of streets. As argued by Serge Salat, this augmented "its capacity for adaptation, and its versatility" through grafting a new scale of the city to the older smaller ones "without eliminating them." (*Law 34-35*)

FURTHER READING:
- **Constantino Doxiadis** - *Ekistics: The Science of Human Settlements*
- **Anthony E.J. Morris** - *History of Urban Form Before the Industrial Revolution*
- **Serge Salat** - *Cities and Forms: On Sustainable Urbanism*
- **Anne Vernez Moudon** - *Built for Change: Neighbourhood Architecture in San Francisco*

CHAPTER 3: Laws of Physical Characteristics - Structure 137

CORDOBA, SPAIN

FORM

40. The main force which shapes human settlements physically is centripetal—that is, the inward tendency towards a close interrelationship of all its parts.

According to Doxiadis, all parts of a settlement seek to be as close to one another as possible, tending to "...form a circle with a centre which exercises a centripetal force." As new pieces are added, they tend to form around the perimeter, each seeking to be as close as possible to the centre.

A brief look at human settlements across history will serve to substantiate this law. From the Sumerian city-state of Ur in Ancient Mesopotamia to the contemporary ideal diagrams of transit-oriented development, Ebenezer Howard's Garden City to Christopher Alexander's "Eccentric Nucleus" pattern, it is clear that the circular, centripetal settlement is a dominant pattern. As such, many smaller settlements tend towards a tight and cohesive shape.

That said, as history also demonstrates, the circular form serves as more of an ideal model, deforming in response to outside forces (*Law 11*) and natural features (*Law 27* and *Law 43*). Moreover, issues related to the dimensions of smaller components that make up the texture of a settlement (*Laws 38-39*) necessarily influence the amount of concentration possible. Even in the era of vast suburban expansion, interstitial waste landscapes and 'in-between dross' we see this tendency, albeit at different scales than those of old settlements. Even a brief look at satellite images of the earth shows interconnected clusters of roughly circular settlements.

It is worth noting that the law implies a 'centre'—that is, something to concentrate around and pull other aspects towards it. Interestingly, Doxiadis suggests that the tendency to form tightly around a nucleus is not as strong within very small settlements of "say, ten or twenty" buildings. At such a scale, central functions have yet to develop.

FURTHER READING:
- **Constantino Doxiadis** - *Ekistics: The Science of Human Settlements*
- **Anthony E.J. Morris** - *History of Urban Form Before the Industrial Revolution*
- **Spiro Kostof** - *The City Shaped*
- **Peter Calthorpe** - *The Next American Metropolis: Ecology, Community, and the American Dream*
- **Hank Dittmar and Gloria Ohland** - *The New Transit Town: Best Practices In Transit-Oriented Development*
- **Ebenezer Howard** - *Garden Cities of To-morrow*
- **Alan Berger** - *Drosscape: Wasting Land in Urban America*
- **NASA** - *View of the World at Night* - https://www.nasa.gov/mission_pages/NPP/news/earth-at-night.html

41. **Although the centripetal force at play ideally appears as settlements of concentric circles, the ultimate forms of settlements are conditioned by curves of equal effort defined dominantly by physical exertion, time, and money. These, in turn are influenced by related factors such as geography, geology, topography, and technology.**

Expanding on the idea put forth in *Law 40*, this law describes the means by which the 'circular ideal' is distorted, transformed and/or modified. He suggests that "effort"—physical exertion, time and money—

142 CHAPTER 3. Laws of Physical Characteristics - Form

MONTSERRAT, SPAIN

conditions the development and growth pattern of a settlement. In keeping with the clarifications made in *Law 27* and *Laws 30-32*, these are also greatly influenced by other issues such as geography, topography, geology and technology.

Through this, Doxiadis provides a number of relevant insights. In a small hillside settlement where the only means of transportation is walking, for example, he suggests that physical exertion is the dominant type of effort determining settlement form. In this case, its ideal circular form will be elongated laterally parallel to the terrain contours since movement is easiest horizontally, as opposed to going up or downhill.

Issues around physical exertion are particularly relevant in contemporary planning, given its focus on walkability. There are many examples of commercial streets that fail as 'walkable' corridors because they were designed perpendicular to the slope direction, instead of in keeping with the contours, for example. In such cases, other mechanical methods of transportation (cars, buses, trams, etc.) that minimize physical effort are required for their survival. Streets like North Vancouver's Lonsdale Avenue in Canada, is an interesting case in point.

In circumstances where inhabitants are wealthy enough to own vehicles that travel at higher speeds (*Law 15*) with minimal effort, Doxiadis states that time becomes the dominant factor shaping a settlement. So, in a settlement where streets are of equal speed, its form will be roughly circular. However, the inclusion of roads that allows twice the speed of the typical street—such as a highway—will deform the shape of the settlement "corresponding to a combination of the time required for the movement both within the normal network and on the highway." This is one of the many issues that account for the transformation of the traditional compact American city to the well known 'sprawling' metropolis of the present, in the wake of national highway networks.

Last, Doxiadis put forward the notion that money— in the form of transportation-related costs—takes a dominant role in the shape of settlements that offer a range of conveyance options (foot, car, public transportation, etc.). This, in turn, leads to more complex forms "since the movement of one part of the population may be determined on the basis of human effort required, another on the time required, and a third on the basis of money needed."

Although to contemporary eyes this law oversimplifies the issue, the fact that physical exertion, time and money can and do directly affect the form of settlement (vis-a-vis transportation) is critically important to remember. Equally significant, and only implied in the above, is the fact that transportation, movement, and access— who can move where, over what amount of time, and how much does it cost—have larger social implications. This, in turn, has a strong relationship to the distribution of wealth across a settlement and one's ability to travel through space. Steven Graham's lucid account of the socio-political issues related to vertical systems in *Vertical: The City from Satellites to Bunkers* (described briefly in *Law 27*) is an important resource around this subject. As is Christine Boyer's *The Power of Place: Urban Landscapes as Urban History*.

FURTHER READING:
- **Constantino Doxiadis** - *Ekistics: The Science of Human Settlements*
- **Anthony E.J. Morris** - *History of Urban Form Before the Industrial Revolution*
- **Spiro Kostof** - *The City Shaped*
- **Stephen Graham** - *Vertical: The City from Satellites to Bunkers*
- **Christine Boyer** - *The Power of Place: Urban Landscapes as Urban History*

42. Linear forces lead to the formation of linear parts of settlements; under certain conditions, this may lead to a linear form of the entire settlement for a certain length only, and after a certain period of time.

Although the main forces acting on a settlement tend towards a circular form (*Law 40*) and issues around effort (*Law 41*) distort and transform this ideal, other uses and functions promote the formation of other shapes of settlement. Of these, linear forces are among the most popular and are often driven by transportation—such as waterways, highways, and streetcar lines. Landscape constraints can also be strong linear forces (*Law 43*).

In *East 40 Degrees: An Interpretive Atlas* Jack Williams describes various linear settlements including the "Railroad Towns" of the 19th century, whose linear forms come from following "the geometry of the tracks." Even more common are the linear 'streetcar suburbs' of North America, whose history and development is well chronicled in Kenneth T. Jackson's *Crabgrass Frontier*.

This process is explicitly represented within Bruce McDonald's *Vancouver: A Visual History*. Consisting of a sequential series of land-use diagrams of over a century of development, the book clearly captures the linear development of Vancouver's early suburbs along the local interurban lines.

FURTHER READING:
- **Constantino Doxiadis** - *Ekistics: The Science of Human Settlements*
- **Hank Dittmar and Gloria Ohland** - *The New Transit Town: Best Practices In Transit-Oriented Development*
- **Jack Williams** - *East 40 Degrees: An Interpretive Atlas*
- **Kenneth T. Jackson** - *Crabgrass Frontier: The Suburbanization of the United States*
- **Bruce McDonald** - *Vancouver: A Visual History*

43. Undetermined forces, usually caused by the form of the landscape, lead to the formation of settlements of undetermined form.

As mentioned briefly in *Law 42*, other factors, especially landscape constraints, play a large roll in shaping a settlement. *Laws 30-32* describe the elements of landscape that affect settlements more explicitly—such as the interaction between geography, topography and geology—as well as other 'softer' variables, such as wind and sun.

Jack Williams highlights various settlements shaped by landscape in *East 40 Degrees: An Interpretive Atlas*, such as the "Alluvial Towns" along the Appalachians that "respond to the shape of stream valleys" and towns of Pennsylvania that "exhibit an order that arises out of the parallel folds or ridges of the Appalachians."

CHAPTER 3: Laws of Physical Characteristics - Form

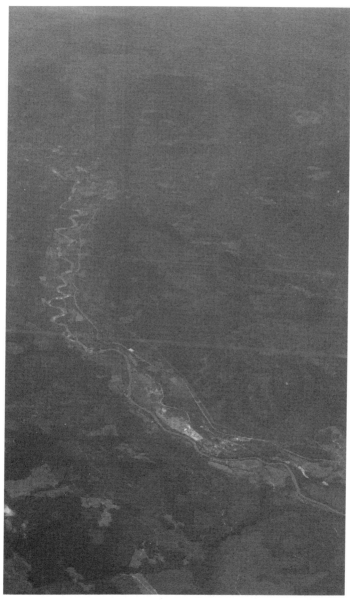

BRITISH COLUMBIA, CANADA

Similarly, Spiro Kostof describes a variety of settlement types largely influenced by landscape features, from the "riverine" settlements with streets that respond to riverbanks, to linear towns—such as Perugia, Italy—that form along the ridges of hills and mountains.

The effects of landscape cut across scale and time. As explained by Anthony Morris, the "linearity of the Forum Romanus was determined mainly by topography." Other 'softer' influences, such as sun and wind, are seen in the form of the ancient Greek city of Priene (Behling) and Winchester, England (P. Kilby), respectively. More recent examples include many informal settlements, such as the favelas of Rio de Janeiro (Graham) that are intricately shaped by the 'unbuildable' slopes of the surrounding mountainside.

Ultimately, the forms of settlements shaped by landscape constraints are variable and 'undetermined'. Still, it is important to recognize that their resulting forms are guided by an inherent logic described by the limitations of geography, topography, geology, sun, and wind.

FURTHER READING:
- **Constantino Doxiadis** - *Ekistics: The Science of Human Settlements*
- **Jack Williams** - *East 40 Degrees: An Interpretive Atlas*
- **Spiro Kostof** - *The City Shaped*
- **Sophia and Stefan Behling** - *Solar Power: The Evolution of Sustainable Architecture*
- **P. Kilby, "Historical Influences Of Wind And Water In Selecting Settlement Sites"** in *Eco-architecture: Harmonisation Between Architecture and Nature* (**C. A. Brebbia**)
- **Anthony E.J. Morris** - *History of Urban Form Before the Industrial Revolution*
- **Stephen Graham** - *Vertical: The City from Satellites to Bunkers*

44. The form of a settlement is determined by a combination of central, linear, and undetermined forces in adjustment to the landscape and in accordance with its positive and negative characteristics.

Laws 40-43 look individually at critical aspects that influence the form of settlements, as a means of focusing on their impacts separately. This law emphasizes their collective effects, and as such is the most realistic description of how settlement form is determined. Although certain determinants take priority under any given circumstance, the number of variables affecting settlement form are always numerous.

The degree to which the factors involved are considered 'positive' or 'negative' is subject to differences in cultural values and needs (*Laws 1-5*). This being the case, settlements come in all shapes and sizes, taking advantage of the often-challenging sites they tend to inhabit. Bernard Rudofsky does well to describe this variety in *Architecture Without Architects: A Short Introduction to Non-Pedigreed Architecture*—from the burrowed settlements within China's loess land and Italian hill towns, to the cliff dwellings of the Dogon in Mali.

This early study has been greatly expanded by those such as Paul Oliver, whose many books offer an exhaustive account of vernacular dwelling types, their corresponding settlements, and the various factors that influenced their form.

It is interesting to note that this law not only speaks to how the form of a settlement develops—such

SAN FRANCISCO, UNITED STATES OF AMERICA

as, the fact that elongated valleys will necessarily bias the creation of elongated settlement or that settlements form along locations where the water is easiest to cross—but also implies that it will occur in a particular sequence. For example, sites that are difficult to build on—such as swamps and deltas—will most likely develop last, with the easiest sites being built up at the outset.

FURTHER READING:
- **Constantino Doxiadis** - *Ekistics: The Science of Human Settlements*
- **Bernard Rudofsky** - *Architecture Without Architects: A Short Introduction to Non-Pedigreed Architecture*
- **Paul Oliver** - *Dwellings: The Vernacular House World Wide* and *Encyclopedia of Vernacular Architecture of the World*
- **Paul Oliver, Marcel Vellinga, Alexander Bridge** - *Encyclopedia of Vernacular Architecture of the World*

45. A settlement grows in the areas of the greatest attraction and least resistance.

In this law, Doxiadis suggests that settlements develop in areas that are the most attractive to their creators—based in needs, values, etc. (*Laws 1-5*)—and offer the path of least resistance to their development (*Law 41*). He also takes the opportunity to concisely summarize *Laws 43-44*:

"....that settlements and their overall functions develop along their main lines of transportation, conditioned by other elements, such as Nature, the type of Society, special functions, the types of transportation used, the cost of movement, etc. These laws also lead to the statement that the growth of settlements take place on the basis of curves of equal

effort, equal time, equal money, etc., or a combination of these, as adjusted to the actual landscape.'

Not addressed in this law, however, are broader 'hidden,' but equally powerful forces, that affect the location and development of human settlements. Keller Easterling's research into the invisible rules that dictate the creation of built environments—such as 'free zones" that exist 'outside' of the local customs authorities for the purposes of encouraging economic activities—are indicative of the complex contemporary mechanisms that dictate "areas of the greatest attraction and least resistance".

FURTHER READING:
- **Constantino Doxiadis** - *Ekistics: The Science of Human Settlements*
- **Keller Easterling** - *Enduring Innocence: Global Architecture and Its Political Masquerades* **and** *Extrastatecraft: The Power of Infrastructure Space*

46. A factor with a direct impact on the form of a settlement is the need for security which may, at times, be even more important than the main centripetal force.

Safety is one of the core physical needs of human beings (*Law 4*) and, by extension, one of the necessary requirements of a settlement. Therefore, according to Doxiadis, security can trump virtually any forces—including the powerful centripetal force (*Law 40-41*)—that influence the form of a settlement. The use of settlements as a means of defense is ancient in origin, creating a wide variety of walled towns, defensive villages and cloaked cities of civilizations past. Authors such as Anthony Morris and Spiro Kostof discuss these at length.

In the past, centripetal forces and the need for security often coincided to create circular settlements. This form minimized wall length to be defended while maximizing the enclosed area. In contrast, the rise of the airplane as a military force fueled the argument for, and subsequent creation of, dispersed settlements that spread away from any central 'core.' This distributed a low-density population across a maximum area, in order to reduce potential casualties.

As such, many architects and planning professionals touted security in promotion of the creating radically decentralized settlement patterns during the mid-twentieth century. This being the case, it advanced the argument for the centrifugal pattern that inflated the distance between spaces so common today. The writing and work of Ludwig Hilberseimer were fundamental in promoting this pattern and his influence is well described by Albert Pope in *Ladders* and Charles Waldheim's *Landscape as Urbanism: A General Theory*.

At the smaller scale, the importance of safety and its impact on the built environment are captured well by Oscar Newman's *Defensible Space*. The book proposes that certain physical attributes and configurations promoting ownership by inhabitants will ensure a safer environment.

At the end of the day, understanding settlements through the point of view of security is important. It forces critical reflection on a variety of issues—from new weaponry and technology (i.e drones) to natural phenomena (earthquakes, etc.)—and their relationship to settlement patterns (nodal vs. linear, compact vs. distributed, etc.).

FURTHER READING:
- **Constantino Doxiadis** - *Ekistics: The Science of Human Settlements*
- **Anthony E.J. Morris** - *History of Urban Form Before the Industrial Revolution*
- **Spiro Kostof** - *The City Shaped*
- **Ludwig Hilberseimer** - *The New Regional Pattern. Industries and Gardens. Workshops and Farms*
- **Albert Pope** - *Ladders*
- **Charles Waldheim** - *Landscape as Urbanism: A General Theory*
- **Oscar Newman** - *Defensible Space*

47. Another force that exercises an influence on the form of a settlement is the tendency towards an orderly pattern.

The predisposition for order is fundamental to human nature. Although Doxiadis neglects to give a specific definition of order, in the context of the built environment, Francis Ching's will certainly suffice. Within his book *Architecture: Form, Space and Order*, Ching establishes order as the "condition of logical, harmonious, or comprehensible arrangement in which each element of a group is properly disposed with reference to other elements and to its purpose." He offers and describes a number of architectural ordering principles accordingly.

Order is also at the root of Christopher Alexander's influential *A Pattern Language*, that cites cross-cultural patterns of settlement. In "The City is not a Tree", however, Alexander importantly defines two different ways of thinking about the order of the city. On one hand, he describes what he believes is the reductionist model of the city as a branched, tree-like diagram that separates and isolates functions

CHAPTER 3: Laws of Physical Characteristics - Form

NETHERLANDS

and activities. On the other, the complex order of the multilayered "semi-lattice" within which uses can interact in an infinite number of ways. In doing so, Alexander highlights the significance of distinguishing between different types of order when it comes to human settlements.

In light of the above, it is clear that all settlements are 'ordered' in some way. However, Doxiadis importantly points out that ordering becomes more difficult to manage—and perceive—as settlements increase in size. As highlighted in Kevin Lynch's seminal *Image of the City*, humans have found ways to navigate large settlements and make them 'legible.' But it remains challenging and a matter of critical research, particularly as settlements continue to expand. In fact, one of the main charges against suburban sprawl is its seemingly 'random' pattern of buildings and spaces.

In keeping with his laws, Doxiadis positions the issue of order between two contradictory extremes: that of the circular 'wheel' based on centripetal forces and that of the grid—the ideal of absolute order. Within this range, he posits, people attempt to make appropriate decisions about the distribution of people, buildings and open spaces. How this is achieved depends on specific circumstances.

FURTHER READING:
- **Constantino Doxiadis** - *Ekistics: The Science of Human Settlements*
- **Francis Ching** - *Architecture: Form, Space and Order*
- **Christopher Alexander** - *A Pattern Language*
- **Christopher Alexander** - *"The City is Not A Tree" Architectural Forum (1965)*
- **Kevin Lynch** - *Image of the City*
- **Nikos A. Salingaros** - *Principles of Urban Structure*

CHAPTER 3: Laws of Physical Characteristics - Form

48. The final form of the settlement depends on the total sum of the forces already mentioned, as well as others such as tradition and cultural factors, which play a greater role in the smaller scales. The final form is a result of the interplay of these primary, secondary, and tertiary forces.

In *Good City Form*, Kevin Lynch states: "City forms, their actual function, and the ideas and values that people attach to them make up a single phenomenon." This not only applies to cities, but to settlements of all types. Unique cultural values and traditions shape the needs of people, as well as their perception of a place. This is elegantly described in "The Beholding Eye: Ten Versions of the Same Scene" within which D.W. Meinig describes the same landscape through the mind's eye of different 'people'.

Given the varied nature of socio-cultural values and traditions and how they interact with the many forces upon them (*Laws 4-5* and *Laws 40-47*), which ones take priority is difficult to predict. A 'suitable' location and/or size of a settlement, for example, differs according to one's unique perception and value system. These variables are more clearly seen in smaller, newer settlements where fewer agents are involved in their shaping. Similarly, fewer physical layers caused by historical growth and development often leaves the initial conditions and solutions more comprehensible in these settlements.

With growth (*Laws 12-13*), time (*Law 14*) and size (*Laws 28-29*), however, settlements develop a thick skin of physical and cultural layers that are complex,

CHAPTER 3: Laws of Physical Characteristics - Form

SURREY, CANADA

plural and even conflicting. This is echoed in Henri Lefebvre's thoughts around spaces interpenetrating and superimposing upon one another over time. Naturally, these are much more difficult to decipher.

FURTHER READING:
- **Constantino Doxiadis** - *Ekistics: The Science of Human Settlements*
- **Kevin Lynch** - *Good City Form*
- **D. W. Meinig**, "The Beholding Eye: Ten Versions of the Same Scene." In *The Interpretation of Ordinary Landscapes: Geographical Essays,* **edited by D. W. Meinig and John Brinckerhoff Jackson**
- **Henri Lefebvre** - *The Production of Space*

49. The form of the settlement is satisfactory only if all the forces of varying importance within it, can be brought into balance physically.

The importance of the internal (dynamic) balance of settlements was discussed in *Laws 22-24*. According to this law, balance must be physically expressed, as the diverse forces acting on a settlement find (dynamic) equilibrium in its material form. As with all major aspects of a settlement, forces are distributed and balanced across different scales. For example, the design of a house is more directly influenced by the forces acting on it at the neighbourhood scale versus those acting at the regional level. This is particularly evident when neighbourhoods support or condemn certain types of housing within their respective areas.

Certain higher level forces do act at smaller scales, however. Using housing as an example once again, municipal level rules and regulations—i.e. zoning, building by-laws—affect the type and distribution of houses in a city, as well as their massing and allowable floor space. These rules can even get into minute details, such as regulating plant choices. The history of regulations and their impacts are well outlined in Emily Talen's *City Rules*.

As a counterpoint to the house, global forces—such as large-scale economic shifts—tend to find their physical scale of influence at a higher level, at least at the outset.

Extremes aside, there is often a limited range within which most forces act physically. In order to remain healthy and viable, they must maintain a certain degree of (dynamic) balance within the form of a settlement.

FURTHER READING:
- **Constantino Doxiadis** - *Ekistics: The Science of Human Settlements*
- **Emily Talen** - *City Rules: How Regulations Affect Urban Form*
- **Eran Ben-Joseph** - *The Code of the City: Standards and the Hidden Language of Place Making*
- **Donald L. Elliott** - *A Better Way to Zone: Ten Principles to Create More Livable Cities*

50. The right form for a human settlement is that which best expresses all the static positions and dynamic movements of humans, animals and machines within its space, while ensuring a healthy ecological setting.

The importance and influence of movement and transportation was touched upon in earlier laws (*Laws 9, 15, 24, 41-42*, and *Law 45*), particularly in relation to certain machines and technologies (cars, airplanes, etc.). In early societies and those without modern technologies, accommodating the movement of animals was critical and was formalized in the shape and dimensions of streets (Hakim). This is seen in many settlements that have maintained their historic physical structure. Settlements with street widths of 7'-8' are not uncommon, for example (Southworth/Ben-Joseph).

What is particularly noteworthy about this law is the reference to both "static positions" and active movements. Doxiadis recognizes that settlements require places of pause and rest, and that these need careful treatment relative to spaces of movement. He gives the example of a central square used for walking, standing and slow circulation, stating that "roads leading to it should not be open, since this will transmit the image of through movement, which is contrary to the function of stability in the square. The perspective leading to such a square should be closed, only then will it truly express the real needs of the square and those who use it."

These sentiments are echoed in Jan Gehl's promotion of the human scale (*Law 25*) and the need to account for different types of movement—moments of rest and motion—in his well-known book *Life Between Buildings*. Arguing that successful public spaces and public life require focusing on the creation of environments that foster "optional activities" (walking, standing, people-watching), his work has influenced the design and transformations of cities globally.

Although the significance of the interaction between settlement and ecology was only beginning to be recognized during Doxiadis' time, its critical importance has come to the foreground quickly, particularly with the rise of climate change. As such, it would be negligent to omit ecological responsibilities when it comes to the "right" form of settlements. I have added this to the original law, accordingly.

The growing relevance and emergence of landscape and ecology in the design of settlements is well captured by Charles Waldheim in *Landscape as Urbanism: A General Theory*. and Randolph Hester's *Design for Ecological Democracy*.

FURTHER READING:
- **Constantino Doxiadis** - *Ekistics: The Science of Human Settlements*
- **Besim Selim Hakim** - *Sidi Bou Sa'id, Tunisia: Structure and Form of a Mediterranean Village*
- **Michael Southworth & Eran Ben-Joseph** - *Streets and the Shaping of Towns and Cities*
- **Jan Gehl** - *Life Between Buildings* and *Cities for People*
- **Jeff Speck** - *The Walkable City: How Downtown Can Save America, One Step at a Time*
- **Charles Waldheim** - *Landscape as Urbanism: A General Theory*
- **Randolph Hester** - *Design for Ecological Democracy*

51. The right form is that which expresses the importance, class, and consequently, the relative scale of every scalar settlement unit and their subdivisions.

Connecting the structural 'texture' of a settlement (*Law 38-39*) to those of physical form, this law speaks to the significance of ensuring that all scales and the elements from which they are composed are

CHAPTER 3: Laws of Physical Characteristics - Form   **163**

BEIJING, CHINA

physically expressed in a settlement. For villages or small cities, for example, he states that the traditional block should be expressed as an important subdividing unit. In doing so, he emphasizes that the relationships are scalar (*Law 0*). Thus, a large city requires a subdivision of a higher order (larger than the traditional block, such as a superblock), while the smaller unit can, and should, remain expressed as its smaller subdivision.

In contrast to Doxiadis, Anne Vernez Moudon argues in *Built for Change* that the building/house is a basic cell of the city, while the lot is basic cell of neighbourhood. Similar to Doxiadis, however, she puts forth the argument that these should be expressed as units of subdivision.

As discussed in *Laws 34-35* and Laws *38-39*, many urbanists interested in complexity and hierarchy theory, such as Nikos Salingaros, N.J. Habraken and Serge Salat, have also pursued this claim. Each of which has described the importance of maintaining, and adding complexity to the existing physical scales of a settlement over time, without erasing earlier structural elements. According to Doxiadis, all of these would consequently find physical expression in a healthy settlement.

FURTHER READING:
- **Constantino Doxiadis** - *Ekistics: The Science of Human Settlements*
- **Anne Vernez Moudon** - *Built for Change: Neighbourhood Architecture in San Francisco*
- **Nikos A. Salingaros** - *Principles of Urban Structure*
- **N.J. Habraken** - *Structure of The Ordinary*
- **Serge Salat** - *Cities and Forms: On Sustainable Urbanism*
- **Kevin Lynch** - *Good City Form*

52. The densities in a settlement, or in any of its parts, depend on the forces which are exercised upon it.

Some will find it curious that Doxiadis refers to density in only the broadest terms. That is, he defines the term to include residential, population, commercial, building, traffic, recreational and institutional, to name a few. This makes sense given that his research cuts across settlements of all scales and that, although the term is most popularly used in contemporary discussions referring to residential uses, density as a topic is much more meaningful when discussed across all spectrums of use and function.

As with all aspects of human settlements, Doxiadis talks about density in the context of the dynamic forces being exerted on it (*Laws 1-4* and *Law 22*). In doing so, he argues that any discussions around densification in the broad sense, must be placed within a larger understanding of the instruments exerting these pressures across all scales. Too frequently, the 'how' of densification, or de-densification, is given with limited or minimal understanding of the 'why'.

From the global perspective, density is much more nuanced and complex than often portrayed. Density responds to the vast array of forces described across all these laws (physical, geographic, cultural, economic, political, for example). The scalar nature of this is understood in reflecting on the 'hidden' infrastructures that concentrates commercial, industrial and residential densities globally towards economic development (described eloquently by Keller Easterling), as well as the small-scale concerns

CUENCA, SPAIN

of local neighbourhood groups fighting against high-rise towers.

Making things more difficult, how a settlement responds to density pressures given its innate inertia (*Law 18*) is a constant challenge. Anthony E.J. Morris, for example, explicitly describes ancient Rome's inability to comprehensively restructure itself due to all the layers of building accrued over time. This, in turn, affected the everyday functioning of the city. Foreshadowing the plight of many contemporary cities, Morris highlights that the density of pedestrian and vehicular traffic was so high by the time of Julius Caesar that he was "forced to ban transport carts from the city during the hours of daylight, with the exception of builders' carts and a few categories of official chariots."

Strategies around limiting transportation densities are mirrored in contemporary cities where congestion charges have been implemented (i.e. London and Singapore) and/or car prohibitions required (such as Mexico's *Hoy No Circula* program)

FURTHER READING:
- **Constantino Doxiadis** - *Ekistics: The Science of Human Settlements*
- **Keller Easterling** - *Enduring Innocence: Global Architecture and Its Political Masquerades* and *Extrastatecraft: The Power of Infrastructure Space*
- **Anthony E.J. Morris** - *History of Urban Form Before the Industrial Revolution*

53. In human settlements formed by a normal process, the pattern of densities changes in a rational and continuous way, according to the scale of the settlement and the functions it serves.

This unassuming law is powerful in its implications. It states that, under a 'normal' process of settlement evolution, density extremes are not possible. Doxiadis defines 'normal' as processes that are allowed to gradually take place over time and respect the natural structure of the settlement (its scale and subdivisions, etc.) with minimal, if any, artificial impositions and limitations.

In his words, it is impossible for any space "which has developed normally, especially at a normal speed, to have an area with a density of inhabitation, functions, investment, and settlement not adjusted to the whole. If, in the texture of the settlement, there is any wasted space, it will tend to be taken over by functions that will fill this area at a required density of people, functions, and investment. If this does not happen, it will usually be due to man-made conditions of legal, administrative or economic significance."

The implications of this principle are far-reaching. It both critiques the contemporary motivations and forces behind settlement building practices that foster density extremes, while simultaneously putting a very heavy burden of responsibility on those who impose "man-made conditions" that curb the gradual processes of settlement evolution.

Sympathetic voices to this law are abundant—from Jane Jacobs' call for gradual 'organic' self-governance and growth to Leon Krier's decree of the skyscraper as built solely for "speculation, or short-term gain, or out of pretentiousness" and in response to the abundance of extremely low density environments that cover the terrain.

Donald Elliot's sharp critique of current zoning practices in *A Better Way to Zone* attempts to address this issue explicitly. His call for "responsiveness" and "predictable flexibility" raises questions around time (short-term vs. long-term interests) and the need to have a system that can adapt to the dynamically changing forces affecting settlements.

There are no easy answers to the challenges put forth by this law and the definition of what constitutes 'normal' is ambiguous, at best. However, the recognition that any artificial imposition on the form of settlements has significant effects across scales and over time is important to keep in mind. As such, critically reflecting on the underlying motivations behind any transformations to "normal processes" must be continuous.

FURTHER READING:
- **Constantino Doxiadis** - *Ekistics: The Science of Human Settlements*
- **Jane Jacobs** - *The Death and Life of Great American Cities*
- **Leon Krier** - *The Architecture of Community*
- **Donald L. Elliott** - *A Better Way to Zone: Ten Principles to Create More Livable Cities*
- **Emily Talen** - *City Rules: How Regulations Affect Urban Form*

54. The satisfaction derived from the services provided by a settlement to its inhabitants depends greatly on the proper density of the settlement.

Referring specifically to the importance of cost-distance and time-distance factors outlined in *Law 37*, Doxiadis' final law connects the latter to the issue of density. In many ways, this principle can be captured by the argument for transit-oriented development and Smart Growth, whereby the density of different uses—transportation types, living, working, recreation—are distributed spatially in sympathy with time and cost constraints.

Recognizing the interconnectedness of these three variables—density, time and cost—Doxiadis describes that a settlement might have a large number of inhabitants, but if they are distributed over a large area relative to themselves and central functions, the services will necessarily be very low.

Furthermore, he states that: "since time- and cost-distances increase with lower densities, the services provided at lower densities decrease in importance." Although there are a variety of different density types (*Law 52*) affected by a diversity of variables, Doxiadis suggests that they all tend to increase and/or decrease at the same time.

FURTHER READING:
- **Constantino Doxiadis** - *Ekistics: The Science of Human Settlements*
- **Peter Calthorpe** - *The Next American Metropolis: Ecology, Community, and the American Dream*
- **Hank Dittmar and Gloria Ohland** - *The New Transit Town: Best Practices In Transit-Oriented Development*
- **Andres Duany, Jeff Speck, and Mike Lydon** - *The Smart Growth Manual*

CHAPTER 3: Laws of Physical Characteristics - Form 171

CUENCA, SPAIN

VANCOUVER, CANADA

Epilogue

Settlements are complex. The more we learn about them, the more elusive they seem. This is especially true now, at a time when rapid settlement construction has spawned new forms of built experiments, big and small. This, in turn, has led many to question the validity of even attempting to decipher 'laws', principles or rules governing human settlements.

Yet, during this time of crisis—when settlements around the world are struggling to adequately respond to social, economic, population and environmental pressures and when the rate of change has increased beyond the point of our ability to adjust accordingly—this trial and error approach will not suffice. The stakes are too high. Ironically, these sentiments are identical to those conveyed by Constantinos Doxiadis in *Ekistics*. At the time, he was confident that developing the scientific approach to settlements outlined in his book would help mobilize the professions that shape the built environment to engage in meaningful research.

Unfortunately, his optimism has not materialized as he had hoped. Although definitive strides have been made in research around human settlements since the time of Doxiadis, its impact on the world has remained very limited, even at a time when the quantity of construction is the highest it has ever been. Instead, narrow and shortsighted perspectives have been allowed to dictate all aspects of human settlements.

This, to my mind, is largely due to the lack of a proper education program that includes mobilizing public opinion. Knowing that the values of inhabitants loomed large in shaping settlements, Doxiadis was explicit in the need for public opinion to be informed by specialized research. Creating a silo of knowledge would do nothing. He quotes Sir Robert Watson-Watt:

When a scientist will not (or cannot) achieve this combination in writing directed to the ordinary reader, he should seek the cooperation of those whose career is based on the serious journalist's trusteeship for the truth in plain language.

To me, this captures the essence of this book. In attempting to question and build on the important research compiled in Ekistics and translate it into everyday language, it embodies the spirit of Doxiadis' work.

With his eye on developing a scientific methodology towards human settlements, Doxiadis was under no delusions that the laws he put forth were definitive. I feel the same way. Although they have solid historical research supporting them, they need to be continuously tested and observed—rejecting or adapting those that fail and building on those that don't.

Doxiadis would be sympathetic to the scientific method as described by American astrophysicist Neil deGrasse Tyson whereby everything must be questioned as a matter of course and evidence needs to be followed, whatever direction it leads—even if it goes against common thought. Only in this way can we hope to create the healthy, livable human settlements we currently long for, and intervene with wisdom and sensitivity.

NETHERLANDS

Acknowledgements

Countless people have inspired, informed and supported this book—some more directly than others, but all equally important. That being the case, I have to apologize in advance for not being able to name everybody individually. For those I miss, hopefully

First and foremost, a warm thanks to the many students I've had over the years at the University of British Columbia in the School of Community and Regional Planning and Environmental Design programs, as well as the Interior Design program at Kwantlen Polytechnic University, who have inspired me with your creativity, curiosity, and constant questions. Your optimism and energy truly drove me to write this in the hopes that you might find it useful as you go about transforming the world.

William Marsh and Doug Paterson stand out as a couple of wonderful people who have informally contributed to this book through their passion for the natural and built worlds, as well as their extreme willingness to share some of their many insights about teaching, design, nature and simply being conscientious, responsible humans beings. I'd be remiss if I did not mention Paul de Greeff who taught with Will and graciously shared his understanding of patterns in the world alongside Jedi Master Marsh. Martin Lewis also deserves a spotlight in this group, as someone who never shies away from calling me out when necessary and sharing his insights about architecture and cities between discussing hockey.

This book would never have come in to existence without Ron Kellett, who introduced me to the work of Doxiadis and sparked my obsession with settlement patterns, in general. This went hand-in-hand with his unpretentious mentoring as I helped teach courses on settlements by his side. Cynthia Girling's support was also critical, as someone who seemed to appreciate my thinking and teaching methods and, as a result, was kind enough to ask me back to teach in the Landscape and Environmental Design programs for so many years.

This opened the door to work alongside other amazing folks, such as Patrick Condon whose work intersected well with mine. Moreover, his incredible ability to explain complex things in simple, accessible ways—a rarity in the academic world—was pivotal not only to my teaching, but also the tone for all my writing: "How would PC say this?" is always at the back of my mind. :)

I can't thank Penny Gurstein and Maged Senbel enough for warmly welcoming me into the School of Community and Regional Planning, after teaching Environmental Design and allowing me to test out my ideas with planning students. This has been crucial in the creation of this book.

Although not directly involved, Matthew Blackett and all his continued support writing for Spacing Magazine and offering the opportunity to be the Editor-in-Chief for Spacing Vancouver, were vital for practicing my writing and getting things out to a broader readership. This also gave me access to countless books—many of which I reviewed—that are referred to in The Laws of Settlements.

I'd also like to thank Charles Montgomery, who kindly invited me to help with some of his Happy City, allowing me a deeper understanding of his amazing research on happiness and cities.

Matt Hern deserves special acknowledgement not only as prolific writer of incredible books, but also for his remarkable generosity in helping edit the book and remind me constantly to say what I need to say and nothing more. His insights and honesty were pivotal in sharpening the message of the book while reducing the word count.

Close friends and family also played their part in the creation of the book and I want to thank my brother and sister-in-law—Dennis and Paola—as well as Kim and Benji Berger for contributing some beautiful photographs of Cuenca & Segovia in Spain and Argentina & Chile, respectively. The amazingly talented Murielle Faifman contributed beautiful images of Paris and Panama City, while the wonderful duo—Emily and Owen—at Point Two Design provided the amazing cover image of the Nile Delta.

I definitely cannot forget Caroline Toth—"Graphic Designer Extraordinaire"—who provided me with essential graphic design tips and suggestions that made all the difference in the look and visual coherence of the book.

Last but not least, a huge thank you to my amazing wife. Not only has she been infinitely patient with my late hours writing and putting this book together, but she was—and continues to be—my most critical and candid editor. She went through and red-lined the book multiple times, and with no thought to ego boosting, ensured that it would be accessible to anybody who picked it up.

SALTA, ARGENTINA

Bibliography

- Abu-Lughod, Janet. "The Islamic City: Historic Myths, Islamic Essence, and Comtemporary Relevance" from *International Journal of Middle East Studies* (1987)
- Aldersea, John and Barbara Hood - *Walhalla, Valley of Gold: a Story of Its People, Places and Its Gold Mines*
- American Planning Association, Frederick R. Steiner, Kent Butler - *Planning and Urban Design Standards*
- Alexander, Christopher - *A Pattern Language*
- Anderson, Darran - *Imaginary Cities*
- Artibise, Yuri - "Urban Fabric: The Form of Cities" - http://yuriartibise.com/urban-fabric/
- Bacon, Edmond - *Design of Cities*
- Batty, Michael - *The New Science of Cities*
- Behling, Sophia and Stefan Behling - *Solar Power: The Evolution of Sustainable Architecture*
- Ben-Joseph, Eran - *ReThinking a Lot: The Design and Culture of Parking*
- Ben-Joseph, Eran - *The Code of the City: Standards and the Hidden Language of Place Making*
- Berelowitz, Lance - *Dream City: Vancouver and the Global Imagination*
- Berger, Alan - *Drosscape: Wasting Land in Urban America*
- Bienart, Julian - MIT course Theory of City Form - https://ocw.mit.edu/courses/architecture/4-241j-theory-of-city-form-spring-2013/index.htm
- Bosselman, Peter - "Images in Motion" in *Representation of Places: Reality and Realism in City Design*
- Brand, Stewart - *How Building Learn: What Happens After They're Built*

- Breasted James Henry - *Ancient times, A History of the Early World: An Introduction to the study of Ancient History and the Career of Early*
- Burdett, Ricky (Editor) and Deyan Sudjic (Editor) - *The Endless City: The Urban Age Project*
- Brillembourg, Alfredo (Editor), et al. - *Torre David: Informal Vertical Communities*
- Calthorpe, Peter - *The Next American Metropolis: Ecology, Community, and the American Dream*
- Calthorpe, Peter and William Fulton - *The Regional City*
- Campanella, Richard - *Bienville's Dilemma: A Historical Georgraphy of New Orleans*
- Campanella, Thomas J. - *The Concrete Dragon: China's Urban Revolution and What it Means for the World*
- Ching, Francis - *Architecture: Form, Space and Order*
- Chow, Renee - *Suburban Space: The Fabric of Dwelling*
- Clague, John and Bob Turner - *Vancouver, City on the Edge: Living with a Dynamic Geological Landscape*
- Clay, Grady - *Close-up: How to Read the American City*
- Crouch, Dora P. - *Spanish City Planning in North America*
- Cullen, Gordon - *The Concise Townscape*
- Davis, Howard - *The Culture of Building*
- Davis, Mike - *Planet of Slums*
- DeKay, Mark and G. Z. Brown - *Sun, Wind, and Light: Architectural Design Strategies*
- Diamond, Jared - *Guns Germs and Steel*
- Diamond, Jared - *Collapse*
- Dittmar, Hank and Gloria Ohland - *The New*

Transit Town: Best Practices In Transit-Oriented Development
- **Dramstad, Wenche, et. al** - *Landscape Ecology Principles in Landscape Architecture and Land-Use Planning*
- **Doxiadis, Constantino A.** - *Ekistics: The Science of Human Settlements*
- **Doxiadis, Constantino A. & J. G. Papaioannou** - *Ecumenopolis: The Inevitable City of the Future*
- **Duany, Andres, et al.** - *The Smart Growth Manual*
- **Easterling, Keller** - *Enduring Innocence: Global Architecture and Its Political Masquerades*
- **Easterling, Keller** - *Extrastatecraft: The Power of Infrastructure Space*
- **Elliott, Donald L.** - *A Better Way to Zone: Ten Principles to Create More Livable Cities*
- **Feddes, Fred** - *A Millennium of Amsterdam: Spatial History of a Marvellous City*
- **Gallion, Arthur** - *The Urban Pattern*
- **Geddes, Patrick** - *Cities in Evolution*
- **Gehl, Jan** - *Cities for People*
- **Gehl, Jan** - *Life Between Buildings*
- **Girling, Cynthia and Ronald Kellett,** *Skinny Streets & Green Neighbourhoods*
- **Goggles (The)** - *Welcome to Pine Point (online story)* - http://pinepoint.nfb.ca/#/pinepoint
- **Glassie, Henry** - *Material Culture*
- **Graham, Stephen** - *Vertical: The City from Satellites to Bunkers*
- **Habraken, N.J.** - *Structure of The Ordinary*
- **Hakim, Besim Selim** - *Sidi Bou Sa'id, Tunisia: Structure and Form of a Mediterranean Village*
- **Hakim, Besim Selim** - *Arabic-Islamic Cities*
- **Hall, Peter** - *Cities in Civilization*
- **Hall, Edward T.** - *The Hidden Dimension*

- Hester, Randolph - *Design for Ecological Democracy*
- Hilberseimer, Ludwig - *The New Regional Pattern. Industries and Gardens. Workshops and Farms*
- Howard, Ebenezer - *Garden Cities of Tomorrow*
- Jackson, Kenneth T. - *Crabgrass Frontier: The Suburbanization of the United States*
- Jacobs, Jane - *The Death and Life of Great American Cities*
- Jacobs, Jane - *The Nature of Economies*
- Jacobs, Allan - *Great Streets*
- Jacobs, Allan - *Looking At Cities*
- Kahneman, Daniel - *Thinking, Fast and Slow*
- Kilby, Peter "Historical Influences Of Wind And Water In Selecting Settlement Sites" in *Eco-architecture: Harmonisation Between Architecture and Nature* (C. A. Brebbia)
- Knox, Paul - *Atlas of Cities*
- Koolhaas, Rem - *GSD Project on the City II - Guide to Shopping*
- Koolhaas, Rem - *GSD Project on the City II - Great Leap Forward*
- Kostof, Spiro - *The City Shaped*
- Kostof, Spiro - *The City Assembled*
- Kunstler, James Howard - *The Geography of Nowhere*
- Lehrer, Jonah. "A Physicist Solves the City," The New York Times, December 17, 2010. - *https://www.nytimes.com/2010/12/19/magazine/19Urban_West-t.html*
- Levine, Robert V. - *A Geography Of Time: On Tempo, Culture, And The Pace Of Life*
- Lynch, Kevin - "The Form of Cities", From Scientific American 190, no 4., 1954

- **Lynch, Kevin** - *Good City Form*
- **Lynch, Kevin** - *Image of the City*
- **Lynch, Kevin and Donald Appleyard** - **View from the Road** (*VIDEO: https://www.youtube.com/watch?v=xP3maTrQZXE*) - **Summary** (*http://contemporarycity.org/2014/03/appleyard-donald-lynch-kevin-myer-john-r/*)
- **McKinsey Global Institute, "Shrinking cities: the rise and fall of global urban populations – mapped" in The Guardian, Nov. 2016.** - *https://www.theguardian.com/cities/gallery/2016/nov/02/global-population-decline-cities-mapped*
- **Marshall, Stephen** - *Streets and Patterns,*
- **Marshall, Stephen** - *Cities Design and Evolution*
- **Marsh, William** - *Environmental Planning*
- **Mattern, Shannon** - *Code and Clay, Data and Dirt: Five Thousand Years of Urban Media*
- **McAlester, Virginia and Lee** - *A Field Guide to American Houses*
- **McDonald, Bruce** - *Vancouver: A Visual History*
- **McHarg, Ian** - *Design With Nature*
- **Meinig, D. W. , "The Beholding Eye: Ten Versions of the Same Scene." In *The Interpretation of Ordinary Landscapes: Geographical Essays*, edited by D. W. Meinig and John Brinckerhoff Jackson**
- **Moore, Jerry D.** - *The Prehistory of Home*
- **Montgomery, Charles** - *Happy City: Transforming Our Live Through Urban Design*
- **Morris, Anthony E.J.** - *History of Urban Form: Before the Industrial Revolution*
- **Moudon, Anne Vernez** - *Built for Change: Neighbourhood Architecture in San Francisco*
- **Mumford, Lewis** - *The City in History: Its Origins, Its Transformations, and Its Prospects*
- **Oldenburg, Ray** - *The Great Good Place*

- Oliver, Paul - *Dwellings: The Vernacular House World Wide*
- Oliver, Paul - *Encyclopedia of Vernacular Architecture of the World*
- Oliver, Paul et al. - *Encyclopedia of Vernacular Architecture of the World*
- Orvell, Mile - *The Death and Life of Main Street: Small Towns in American Memory, Space, and Community*
- Podolyak, Pavel - " Optimal City Population Size" The Pragmatist, November 30, 2014 - *http://pavelpodolyak.blogspot.com/2014/11/optimum-city-population-size.html*
- Pope, Albert - *Ladders*
- Pentland, Alex - *Social Physics*
- Pirenne, Henri - *Medieval Cities: Their Origins and the Revival of Trade*
- Punter, John - *The Vancouver Achievement: Urban Planning and Design*
- Jackson, J.B. "The Stranger's Path." *In Landscape in Sight*. London: Yale University Press.
- Johnson, Steve - *Emergence: The Connected Lives of Ants, Brains, Cities, and Software*
- Rapoport, Amos - *House Form and Culture*
- Reps, John - *The Making of Urban America: A History of City Planning in the United States*
- Rose, Jonathan F. P. - *The Well-Tempered City*
- Rudofsky, Bernard - *Architecture Without Architects: A Short Introduction to Non-Pedigreed Architecture*
- Sadik-Khan, Janette & Seth Solomonow - *Street Fight: Handbook for the Urban Revolution*
- Salat, Serge - *Cities and Forms: On Sustainable Urbanism*
- *Shrinking Cities* - *http://www.shrinkingcities.com/kultur_schrumpfen.0.html?&L=1*

- **Salingaros, Nikos A.**, *Principles of Urban Structure*
- **Solà-Morales, Manuel de** - *Ten Lessons On Barcelona*
- **Sorensen, André**, *The Making of Urban Japan: Cities and Planning from Edo to the Twenty First Century*
- **Southworth, Michael & Eran Ben-Joseph** - *Streets and the Shaping of Towns and Cities*
- **Speck, Jeff** - *The Walkable City: How Downtown Can Save America, One Step at a Time*
- **Stavros, Matthew & Ronald G. Knapp**, *Kyoto: An Urban History of Japan's Premodern Capital*
- **Stilgoe, John** - *Outside Lies Magic*
- **Suisman, Doug** - *Los Angeles Boulevards: Eight X-rays of the Body Public*
- **Tainter, Joseph** - *Collapse of Complex Societies*
- **Talen, Emily** - *City Rules: How Regulations Affect Urban Form*
- **Tschumi, Bernard** - *Red is not a Colour*
- **Venturi Robert & Denise Scott Brown** - *Learning From Las Vegas*
- **Vuchic, Vukan R.** - *Urban Transit Systems and Technology*
- **Waldheim, Charles** - *Landscape as Urbanism: A General Theory*
- **Walker, Jarrett** - *Human Transit: How Clearer Thinking about Public Transit Can Enrich Our Communities and Our Lives*
- **West, Geoffrey - The Surprising Math of Cities and Corporations** https://www.ted.com/talks/geoffrey_west_the_surprising_math_of_cities_and_corporations/transcript?language=en#t-707000

- **West, Geoffrey** - *Scale: The Universal Laws of Growth, Innovation, Sustainability, and the Pace of Life in Organisms, Cities, Economies, and Companies*
- **Williams, Jack** - *East 40 Degrees: An Interpretive Atlas*
- **Whyte, Lancelot Law & Albert G. Wilson, & Donna Wilson (Editors)** - *Hierarchical structures*
- **Whyte, William H.** - *The Social Life of Small Urban Spaces*

MACHU PICCHU, PERU

Index

A

A Better Way to Zone 169
Abu-Lughod, Janet 33, 48
Access 144
Acropolis 66
Adaptation 61
A Geography Of Time 94
Agriculture 51
Airplane 66
Alexander, Christopher 27, 91, 140, 154, 156
Amortize 72, 83
Anderson, Darran 33
Angkor Wat 101
Appleyard, Donald 66
Architecture: Form, Space and Order 154, 156
Architecture Without Architects 109, 110, 118, 149, 151
Aristotle 38
Automobile 66

B

Bacon, Edmund 91
Balance 54, 85, 86, 89, 90, 92, 159
Balance, dynamic 87
Balance, homeostatic 89
Balance, internal 85
Barcelona 35, 53, 62
Barcino 62
Behling, Stefan & Sophia 148
Ben-Joseph, Eran 66, 161
Berelowitz, Lance 63, 184
Berlin 78
Bienart, Julian 101
Body 92
Boyer, Christine 144
Brand, Stewart 42, 75
Breasted, James 114
Brown, G.Z. 27, 109
Built for Change 28, 80, 122, 123, 134, 136, 164

C

Campanella, Thomas J. 54, 90
Çatalhöyük 80, 101
Cell 164
Centrifugal 153
Centripetal 140, 141, 152, 153, 156
Ceology 114
China 54
Ching, Francis 154
Chow, Renee 29, 91
Circular 140, 141, 143, 145, 153
City Rules 160
Class, settlement 116
Climate 109, 110
Co-dependence 26, 51, 53, 98, 115, 116, 123, 126
Collapse 35, 36, 83, 86
Compact 144, 153
Complexity 35, 125
Concentric 141
Congestion 167
Connectivity 94
Corbusier 66, 129
Core Needs 38, 39
Core physical needs 32, 36, 38, 39, 70, 152
Cost-distance 130, 170
Crabgrass Frontier 145, 146
Creation 89, 101, 128
Cullen, Gordon 64
Culture 109

D

Davis, Mike 87
Death 44, 48, 50, 70, 72, 75, 78, 80, 82
Decentralized 153
Decline 55, 56, 70, 75, 100
Defensible Space 36, 153
DeKay, Mark 27, 109

Densification 165
Densities 165, 167, 170
Density 165, 168, 170
Design for Ecological Democracy 162
Detroit 78, 100, 110
Development 86, 89, 157
Diamond, Jared 51, 83, 86
Disease 32
Dispersed 153
Distributed 153, 159
Diversity 35, 170
Dogon (Mali) 149
Dramstad, Wenche 91
Dusseldorf 100
Dynamic 62, 90, 107, 115, 159, 160, 165, 169

E

East 40 Degrees: An Interpretive Atlas 28, 98, 100, 145, 146, 148
Easterling, Keller 54, 152, 165
Ecology 162
Ecumenopolis 26, 107
Effort 152
Ekistic Logarithmic Scale 106
Ekistic Units 26
Elliot, Donald 169
Equilibrium 54, 159
Evolution 89, 168
Extinction 50, 70

F

Fabric, physical 75, 122
Fabric, urban 77
Favelas 102, 109, 148
Folk architecture 71
Forces 32, 33, 78, 80, 86, 89, 90, 127, 140, 141, 145, 146, 152, 153, 154, 156, 157, 159, 160, 165, 168

Forces, primary 157
Forces, secondary 55, 157
Forces, tertiary 157
Form 140, 143, 145, 146, 148, 151, 153, 154, 157, 159, 160, 162
Fractal 127, 129
Functions 114, 115, 116, 117, 123, 128, 145, 168, 170

G

Garden City 106, 140
Gehl, Jan 91, 92, 161
Geographic Information System (GIS) 130
Geography 51, 53, 98, 100, 101, 109, 114, 115, 117, 141, 143, 146, 148
Geology 100, 101, 102, 109, 114, 141, 143, 146, 148
Glassie, Henry 71
Good City Form 157
Graham, Stephen 54, 63, 87, 102, 144, 148
Grid 129, 156
Growth 58, 117, 143, 157

H

Habraken, N.J. 43, 91, 125, 126, 164
Hakim, Besim 64, 67
Hall, Edward T. 92
Happiness 36, 38, 39
Happy City 38, 39, 94
Hester, Randolph 162
Hierarchy 123, 125, 126, 127, 128, 129, 164
High order function 130
High order settlement 125, 128
Highway 62, 66, 90, 129, 143, 144
Highways 145
Hilberseimer, Ludwig 153
Homeostasis 87, 94
homeostatic 89, 94

Hong Kong 53
Howard, Ebenezer 106, 140

I

Image of the City 156
Industrial city 110
Industry 98
Inertia 78, 79
Informal 87
Informal Community 74
Infrastructure 59, 165
Instability 44
Interactions 32
Interdependence 118, 127
Interurban 146
Investment 53, 54, 168
Islamic City 33, 48
Istanbul 35

J

Jackson, John Brinckerhoff 67
Jackson, Kenneth T. 145
Jacobs, Allan B. 42
Jacobs, Jane 42, 78, 91, 94, 169

K

Kahneman, Daniel 83
Kilby, P. 148
Kniffen, Jan 74
Knox, Paul 53
Koestler, Arthur 123
Koolhaas, Rem 90
Kostof, Spiro 125, 148, 152
Krier, Leon 169
Kunstler, James Howard 82

L

Ladders 153
Landscape 145, 146, 148, 152, 153, 162
Landscape as Urbanism: A General Theory 153, 154, 162, 190
Land-use 94, 146
Las Vegas 67
Laws of the Indies 63
Leavenworth, WA 53
Lefebvre, Henri 159
Leonardo 106
Levine, Robert V. 94
Life Between Buildings 161
Lifecycle 77
Lifestyle Centres 74
Linear 145, 148, 153
Location 98, 114, 115, 117, 157
London (England) 53, 167
Lonsdale Avenue (North Vancouver, Canada) 143
Los Angeles 63
Los Angeles Boulevards 63
Lower order settlement 125, 128
Low order function 130
Lynch, Kevin 38, 48, 66, 87, 156, 157

M

Machu Picchu 80, 101
Main Street 51, 122
Maintenance 41, 72
Manchester 110
Maya 35
McAlester, Virginia & Lee 71
McDonald, Bruce 146
McHarg, Ian 91
Medieval Cities 51, 70, 75
Meinig, Donald W. 157
Memphis (Egypt) 80

Memphis (Tennessee) 115, 116
Mexico 167
Middle Ages 100
Military 153
Milton Keynes 106
Money 141, 144
Montgomery, Charles 38, 39, 94
Morris, Anthony 36, 64, 75, 114, 148, 152, 167
Morrish, William 33
Movement 64, 143, 144, 151, 160, 161

N

Natural setting 98
Needs 32, 35, 41, 70, 80, 100, 106, 109, 157
Neighbourhood 159, 164, 167
Neolithic 114
Nested hierarchy 125
Network 75, 125, 144
Newman, Oscar 153
New York 53
NIMBY 79
Nodal 153
North Vancouver 143

O

Oldenburg, Ray 122
Oliver, Paul 71
Order 154, 156

P

Pattern Language 15, 27, 29, 91, 154, 156
Perception 66
Physical characteristics 97
Physical exertion 141, 143, 144
Pirenne, Henri 27, 51, 56, 75, 77, 100
Podolyak, Pavel 106

Pope, Albert 153
Population size 114, 116, 117
Priene (Greece) 148
Process 55, 168
Promenade architecturale 66

R

Rapoport, Amos 109
Rates of change 42
Regulations 159
Renaissance 51
Renewal 48, 86
Reps, John 64
Resilience 125
Resistance 151
Resort Municipalities 53
Resource-based towns 70
Resources 44, 98
Revival 80
Rhodes, Robin Francis 66
Role 117
Roman Empire 35, 56, 70, 75, 77
Rome 63, 77
Rudofsky, Bernard 109

S

Sadik-Khan, Janette 62, 64, 189
Safety 38, 152
Salat, Serge 29, 64, 125, 126, 127, 129, 164
Salingaros, Nikos 29, 125, 126, 127, 164
Scalar 162, 165
Scalar units 122, 123, 126
Scalar units, Ekistic 106
Scale 110, 127, 148, 159, 160, 162, 168
Scale, human 92, 94
Scales 90, 91, 92, 106, 122, 126, 129, 159, 164, 165

Scales, nested 126
Scott Brown, Denise 66
Secondary forces 55
Security 152, 153
Self-governance 169
Semi-lattice 156
Senses 92
Serial Vision 64
Services 170
Settlements 26
   Access 144
   Adaptation 61
   Amortize 72, 83
   As process 48, 50, 55
   Balance 54, 85, 86, 89, 90, 92, 159
   Balance, dynamic 87
   Balance, homeostatic 89
   Balance, internal 85
   Cell 164
   Centrifugal 153
   Centripetal 140, 141, 152, 153, 156
   Circular 140, 141, 143, 145, 153
   Class, settlement 116
   Climate 109, 110
   Co-dependence 26, 51, 98, 115, 116, 123, 126
   Co-dependent 98
   Collapse 35, 36, 83, 86
   Compact 144, 153
   Complexity 125
   Concentric 141
   Congestion 167
   Control 43
   Core Needs 38, 39
   Core physical needs 32, 36, 38, 152
   Cost-distance 130, 170
   Creation 32, 82, 89, 101, 128
   Culture 109
   Death 44, 48, 50, 70, 75, 78, 80, 82

Decentralized 153
Decline 55, 56, 70, 75, 100
Densification 165
Densities 165, 167, 170
Density 165, 168, 170
Development 31, 48, 82, 86, 89, 157
Dispersed 153
Distributed 153, 159
Diversity 170
Dynamic 62, 90, 107, 115, 159, 160, 165, 169
Ecumenopolis 107
Effort 152
Equilibrium 54, 159
Evolution 89, 168
Extinction 50, 70
Fabric, physical 75, 122
Fabric, Urban 77
Forces 32, 33, 78, 80, 86, 89, 90, 127, 140, 141, 145, 146, 152, 153, 154, 156, 157, 159, 160, 165, 168
Forces, primary 157
Forces, Primary 32, 55
Forces, secondary 55, 56, 157
Forces, tertiary 157
Form 140, 143, 145, 146, 148, 151, 153, 154, 157, 159, 160, 162
Functions 114, 115, 116, 117, 123, 128, 145, 168, 170
Geography 51, 53, 98, 100, 101, 109, 114, 115, 117, 141, 143, 146, 148
Geology 100, 101, 102, 109, 114, 141, 143, 146, 148
Grid 129, 156
Growth 58, 117, 143, 157
Hierarchy 123, 125, 126, 127, 128, 129, 164
High order function 130
High order settlement 125, 128
Industry 98
Inertia 78, 79
Informal 74
Infrastructure 59, 165

Instability 44
Interconnection 29
Interdependence 118, 127
Investment 53, 54, 168
Land-use 94, 146
Lifecycle 77
Lifespan 77
Linear 145, 148, 153
Location 98, 114, 115, 117, 157
Lower order settlement 125, 128
Low order function 130
Main Street 122
Maintenance 41
Money 141, 144
Movement 64, 143, 144, 151, 160, 161
Natural setting 98
Needs 32, 35, 70, 80, 100, 106, 109, 157
Neighbourhood 159, 164, 167
Neolithic 114
Nested hierarchy 125
Network 75, 125, 144
Nodal 153
Order 154, 156
Perception 66
Physical characteristics 97
Physical exertion 141, 143, 144
Population size 114, 116, 117
Process 168
Rates of change 42
Regulations 159
Renewal 48, 86
Resilience 125
Resistance 151
Resources 44, 98
Revival 80
Role 117
Safety 38, 152
Scalar 26, 78, 162, 165

Scalar unit 122
Scalar units 123, 126
Scalar units, Ekistic 106
Scale 110, 127, 148, 159, 160, 162, 168
Scale, human 92, 94
Scales 90, 91, 92, 122, 126, 129, 159, 164, 165
Scales, nested 126
Security 152, 153
Services 170
Shells 75, 78
Size 59, 61, 100, 106, 107, 109, 110, 114, 116, 117, 129, 156, 157
Size, Optimal 107
Slum 74
Speed 64, 66, 67, 91, 143
Sprawl 156
Stabilization 90
Static 160
Street 66, 129, 143, 148, 161
Structure 43, 122, 123, 125, 168
Suburb 67, 145, 146, 156
Survival 51
Technology 32, 100, 101, 102, 109, 114, 118, 141, 143, 153, 161
Texture 162
Time 55, 64, 75, 91, 94, 115, 127, 130, 141, 144, 145, 157, 167, 169, 170
Time-distance 130, 170
Topography 98, 100, 101, 109, 114, 117, 141, 143, 146, 148
Town 51, 70, 78, 82, 98, 145, 146, 152
Town, medieval 51
Town, Themed 53
Trade 98, 115
Transportation 144, 145, 151, 160, 167, 170
Travel time 130
Unforeseen functions 35
Unit 123, 164

    Values 32, 55, 70, 75, 77, 101, 102, 109, 151, 157
    Village 152
    Walk 143
    Walkability 143
    Wealth 144
    Zoning 169
Shells 75, 78
Shopping mall 51, 74, 82
Shrinking Cities 110
Sidi Bou Sa'id 64
Silk Road 33
Singapore 167
Size 59, 61, 100, 106, 107, 109, 110, 114, 116, 117, 129, 156, 157
Size, Optimal 107
Skara Brae 80
Slum 74
Smart Growth 170
Solomonow, Seth 62, 64, 189
Southworth, Michael 66, 161
Speculation 169
Speed 64, 66, 67, 91, 143
Sprawl 156
Squamish, British Columbia 116
Stabilization 90
Static 160, 161
Stilgoe, John 82
Street 66, 129, 143, 148, 161
Streetcar 145
Street geometry 94
Structure 43, 122, 123, 125, 168
Suburb 67, 145, 146, 156
Suisman, Doug 63
Sun 146, 148
Sun, Wind, and Light: Architectural Design Strategies 27, 109, 110
Supermarket 128
Survival 51

T

Tainter, Joseph 35, 83
Talen, Emily 160
Technology 32, 100, 101, 102, 109, 114, 118, 141, 143, 153, 161
Teotihuacán 101
Texture 162
The Goggles 44
The Power of Place: Urban Landscapes as Urban History 144
Third place 122
Time 64, 75, 91, 94, 115, 127, 130, 141, 144, 145, 157, 167, 169, 170
Time-distance 130, 170
Topography 98, 100, 101, 109, 114, 117, 141, 143, 146, 148
Torre David 74, 75
Town 51, 55, 70, 78, 82, 98, 145, 146, 152
Town, medieval 51
Town, Themed 53
Trade 32, 33, 98, 115
Transit-oriented development 92, 170
Transportation 66, 91, 144, 145, 151, 160, 167, 170
Travel time 130
Tunisia 64
Tyson, Neil deGrasse 175

U

Unit 123, 164
United Arab Emirates 54
Ur (Mesopotamia) 140

V

Values 32, 55, 70, 75, 77, 101, 102, 109, 151, 157
Vancouver: A Visual History 146
Vancouver, Canada 56, 116
Venturi, Robert 66

Vernacular architecture 71
Vernez Moudon, Anne 28, 29, 79, 80, 122, 123, 134, 136, 164
Vertical: The City from Satellites to Bunkers 54, 55, 63, 64, 67, 89, 102, 110, 144, 145, 148
Vienna 35, 152
Village 152

W

Waldheim, Charles 153, 162
Walhalla, Australia 78
Walk 66, 67, 92, 94, 128, 143
Walkability 143
Walker, Jarrett 91, 130
Walking distance, ten-minute 92, 94
Wealth 144
West, Geoffrey 58, 61
Whistler, BC 53
Whyte, Lancelot Law 123
Williams, Jack 28, 98, 145, 146
Wilson, Albert G. 123
Wilson, Donna 123
Winchester (England) 148
Wind 146, 148

Z

Zoning 159, 169

BRITISH COLUMBIA, CANADA

Printed in Poland
by Amazon Fulfillment
Poland Sp. z o.o., Wrocław